06·09
19.95

Withdrawn

BULGARIA

BULGARIA

STEVEN OTFINOSKI

☑® Facts On File, Inc.

Bulgaria

Facts On File, Inc.
11 Penn Plaza
New York NY 10001

Library of Congress Cataloging-in-Publication Data

Otfinoski, Steven.
    Bulgaria / Steven Otfinoski.
        p.   cm. — (Nations in transition)
    Includes bibliographical references and index.
    Summary: Examines the people, religion, daily life, politics,
culture, history, and geography of Bulgaria, emphasizing its
transition from a Communist to a free nation.
    ISBN 0-8160-3705-1
    1. Bulgaria—History—1990——Juvenile literature.
[1. Bulgaria.]   I. Title.   II. Series.
DR93.42.086   1998
949.903—dc21   98-10577

Facts On File books are available at special discounts when purchased in bulk quantities for businesses, associations, institutions, or sales promotions. Please call our Special Sales Department in New York at 212/967-8800 or 800/322-8755.

You can find Facts On File on the World Wide Web at http://www.factsonfile.com

Text design by Cathy Rincon
Cover design by Nora Wertz
Illustrations on pages 5 and 45 by Dale Williams

Printed in the United States of America.

MP   FOF   10 9 8 7 6 5 4 3 2 1

This book is printed on acid-free paper.

*T*o Elena Atanassova and all the other young people of Bulgaria, at home and abroad, who care about their country and its future

Contents

Note on Pronunciations

Throughout the text, pronunciations are given for Bulgarian words and names, but not for terms in Russian or other foreign languages.

Following is a list of symbols or letter combinations used for the vowel sounds:

a—as in Sar*ah*
o—as in sh*o*t
oo—as in j*u*bilee
e—as in *e*lephant
i—as in sh*e*
u—as in g*u*ts
ei—as in n*ei*ghbor
ai—as in *eye*
For some consonants:
j—as in de*j*a vu
dj—as in *J*ack

Syllable that is stressed is in uppercase letters.

1

An Introduction to the Land and Its People

*T*ens of thousands of demonstrators flooded the streets of central Sofia (SO-fi-ya), Bulgaria's ancient capital city. It was the eighth straight day of protest and the temperatures, as they were throughout Eastern Europe that winter, were mercilessly bitter. Yet the demonstrators were not deterred by the frigid cold. Many carried signs with messages as bleak as the winter landscape. "I am Bulgarian, I am hungry" and "Future without misery." Many chanted "Red trash" at the warmly dressed Socialist leaders who watched the demonstration with growing anxiety.

Although the politicians had agreed to relinquish their power in the face of Bulgaria's worst economic crisis in a decade, they were in no hurry to do so. They said they would stay in office until elections, which were scheduled in about a year. The demonstrators found their stalling tactics intolerable. For them, the Socialist government had had its chance to improve living conditions and had failed miserably. "Can we wait 500 days?" opposition leader Ivan Kostov (i-VAN KOS-tof) cried out to the crowd. "Never, never!" was the emphatic reply.

This tumultuous scene could have taken place in 1989 as the fires of freedom broke out across Eastern Europe. But it did not. The date was January 1997. While most of Eastern Europe had come to terms with the Communist past and was on a steady, if often bumpy, road to a democratic system of government and a free-market economy, Bulgaria had stayed mired in the past. Bulgaria's Communist leaders had stepped down, changed their party name to "Socialist," and returned to power in free elections. Turned out by voters for a brief time, they won reelection in 1994 and over the next two years managed to lead Bulgaria further down the path of economic disaster and near political chaos.

"We should have improved," said Anna Penkova (pen-KO-va), who cut down trees with her son for winter fuel because they couldn't afford heating oil in their village home. "But instead we are going down and down. Many people this winter will go up. They will die and go to heaven."

And it wasn't only the poor who were feeling life's miseries. "Our situation is unbearable," says Zhana Boetri (JA-na bo-E-tri), a teacher. "We're supposed to be middle-class Bulgarians, but you can't call us that anymore. We had a car, but it was stolen last year."

The word *transition* has more than one meaning for this struggling Balkan nation. Emerging from Communist domination is only one transition Bulgaria must make as the 20th century draws to a close. One of Europe's poorest countries, it is still in the midst of making the larger transition from centuries of political, economic, and social backwardness to modern nationhood. "The sense that Bulgaria needed to do fifty years' worth of catching up made the transition to democracy even harder," observed writer Pamela Mitova (MI-to-va).

Its days of glory as a major player in Eastern Europe in the distant past, Bulgaria has spent most of the last 600 years under the yoke of two masters—the Turks, whom they hated, and the Russians, whom they embraced as liberators. It was the Russians who freed Bulgaria from the harsh rule of the Ottoman Turks in 1878, but then in turn made the Bulgarians their vassals.

Bulgaria's relationship with the Soviet Union during the 40 years of Soviet domination was a unique one. Until the 1980s, dissent against the Communist regime was practically nonexistent, although there was plenty to dissent against. Half a century of Communist rule had disrupted traditions, broken the people's spirit, and polluted their once pristine land. On the other hand, the Soviets brought Bulgaria into the 20th century, industrialized the country, improved agriculture, and boosted the standard of living for millions of people.

The most loyal of the Soviet satellite countries, Bulgaria remains as remote to most Westerners as the moon. "The average European knows

These strange rock formations stand guard over an ancient Roman fortress near the town of Belogradhik. The stark beauty of this ancient land is only now being revealed to the West after decades of Communist isolation. (UPI/Corbis-Bettmann)

only that Bulgaria was Moscow's most loyal satellite," notes Bulgarian historian Bojidar Dimitrov (bo-ji-DAR di-mi-TROF), "that its military industry was selling weapons all over the globe, and that it looked as if it had something to do with drug trafficking and the attempt to assassinate the Pope."

Its very isolation from Western Europe and the United States has made Bulgaria all the more reluctant to embrace Western ways, although young Bulgarians are as attracted to the West as the youth of Poland, Hungary, and the Czech Republic are.

"It's a question of where we are," says Bulgarian filmmaker Vladimir Andreev (vla-di-MIR an-DRE-ef). "Geographically we're in Europe, but there is quite a strong tendency, as in Russia, to believe that we're something special with our own history and problems, and that the principles of Europe can't be exactly implanted here."

That Bulgaria is indeed something special is only beginning to be recognized by the West. As its ancient cities, resilient people, and colorful folk arts and music are being opened to the West, Westerners are learning who the Bulgarians are and the crisis they are facing becomes more compelling. A "future without misery" may be an optimistic wish in light of the misery that has dogged Bulgaria through much of its history.

Small Country, Mixed Geography

Bulgaria is located in southeastern Europe on the Balkan Peninsula, which it shares with Romania, the republics of the former Yugoslavia, Albania, Greece, and European Turkey. It is a small country, a little bigger than the state of Tennessee, with a population of some 8.5 million. About 86 percent of the population is Bulgarian, while another 10 percent are ethnic Turks who have lived here for hundreds of years. The remaining 4 to 5 percent of people are mostly Gypsies, Armenians, Russians, Macedonians, and Greeks.

The Gypsies, who call themselves Romanies, are a nomadic people originally from India who live throughout Europe. The Armenians, Russians, and Greeks have immigrated here from their respective homelands. The Macedonians are descendants of a once great country located south of Bulgaria that was once the home of the conqueror Alexander the

Great. Over the centuries, Macedonia was absorbed by Bulgaria, Greece, and the former Yugoslavia.

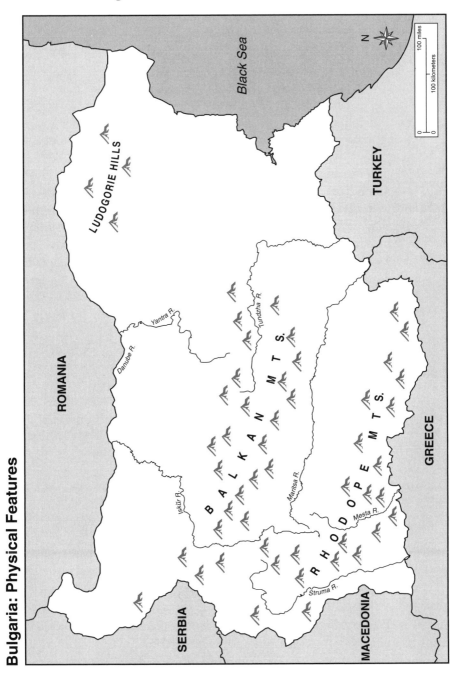

Bulgaria: Physical Features

National Character

"We Bulgarians are such people—we suffer and do nothing," With these words Maria Vaseva, (VA-se-va) an unemployed electronics specialist, sums up what she considers the dark side of the Bulgarian national character. At the same time, this deep strain of stoicism has helped this Balkan country to survive countless foreign invasions and occupations.

Apathy can be seen as a national malaise, particularly in the seven years since the collapse of communism. But if the Bulgarians' tolerance for oppression seems high, so is their love of work, thoughtfulness to others, and love of people, especially family.

Family is everything to Bulgarians. They lavish care on their children, take in the elderly, and are close to brothers, sisters, and cousins. Most Bulgarians believe in hard work, and they are always busy. As one old Bulgarian proverb states: "Work left for later is finished by the Devil."

While work is important, so is play. Bulgarians of all classes love to sing and dance. Telling stories and jokes is a national pastime and conversation is as natural as breathing. Nowhere is this more apparent than on a Bulgarian train. Perfect strangers who start a journey in the same railroad car often end up telling each other their life story before arriving at their destination.

Although long considered in the backwater of Europe, Bulgarians pride themselves on being well educated. Reading is a favorite pastime, whether it be newspapers, magazines, or books.

While religion is important to Bulgarians, faith for many does not run deep. Religion is part of their national spirit, and their allegiance to the Bulgarian Orthodox Church is as much an expression of fervent patriotism as it is of religious faith.

Bulgaria is bounded to the north by Romania, to the east by the Black Sea, which provides it with a 175-mile coastline, to the south by Greece and Turkey, and on the west by Serbia and Macedonia.

Although small, Bulgaria has a surprising variety of land forms. More than two-thirds of the country is covered with plains and plateaus, while nearly a quarter of the remaining land is mountainous. Bulgaria's mountains have been both a blessing and a curse. They have isolated villages, cutting them off from the rest of the world for centuries. They have also

Good and bad, the national character of the Bulgarians has both held them back from new challenges and sustained them when faced with insurmountable ones.

The joy of living, even in hard times, is captured in the smile of this peasant woman. The Bulgarian national character is a mixture of optimism and apathy. (Sonja Iskov/Impact Visuals)

provided Bulgarian freedom fighters through history with a safe haven from the countless invaders who have attacked and occupied their land. From north to south, there are four main geographical regions. The Danube River, which marks most of its northern border with Romania, forms a huge plateau that extends south to the Balkan Mountains. The Danube, Europe's second-longest river, is a far cry from "the beautiful blue Danube" of the famous Strauss waltz. It is more yellow than blue from silt, sand, and industrial pollution. Yet the Danubian Plateau contains

Bulgaria's most fertile soil, which produces wheat, corn, sugar beets, tobacco, and sunflowers.

The Balkan Mountains, running from east to west, nearly slice the country in half. These ancient peaks give the entire peninsula its name, and the Bulgarians refer to them as "Stara Planina" (STA-ra pla-ni-NA) or "Old Mountains." They are composed of granite and crystalline rock and contain deposits of some minerals, although they are better known for the timber of their thick forests.

Below the Balkans are the Lowlands and Transitional Mountains with more fertile valleys, including the Valley of Roses, where one of Bulgaria's most famous exports, rose oil, is made (see boxed feature, chapter 7).

Further south, to the west, marking Bulgaria's border with Greece, are the Rhodope (ro-DO-pi) Mountains, fabled in Bulgarian folklore and song. They are rich in timber and minerals and contain the country's highest point, Musala (moo-sa-LA) Peak, which rises 9,596 feet (2,924 m).

Equally legendary is the Black Sea to the east, named for the dark hue created by storm clouds and fog in the winter, or for the dark demons that once inhabited its shores, according to Bulgarian folklore. But most of the year the Black Sea is bright and crystal clear. In the summer months, it attracts 1.5 million vacationers who enjoy its sunny beaches and comfortable resorts. It remains the center of Bulgaria's thriving tourist industry.

Bulgaria's varied terrain creates a wide range of climactic conditions. Summers in the north tend to be humid; in the south, dry. Most of the country enjoys mildly cold winters and the only heavy snowfall is in the mountain regions.

Bulgaria is plagued by one natural disaster—earthquakes. Sixteen major quakes have struck in this century, most of them in the north and the west Rhodopes.

Land of Contrasts

Bulgaria's culture is as full of contrasts as is its geography. The ancient and the modern stand side by side. In Sofia, the remains of a tower built nearly 2,000 years ago by the Romans sits in the basement of a modern department store. The cab that takes young people to Eddy's Tex-Mex Diner, one of the capital's hottest nightspots, may have its hood adorned with a collar of beads meant to ward off the evil eye. One of the most celebrated of contemporary Bulgarians is the artist Christo (HRI-sto), who creates strange artworks by wrapping monuments, buildings, and natural landscapes with plastics and fabrics.

Poor in many things, Bulgaria is a land rich in physical beauty, history, culture, and the spirit of its people. Hopefully the difficult transitions it is now facing will not rob it of these riches.

NOTES

p. 1   "I am Bulgarian, . . ." *Connecticut Post,* January 15, 1997, p. A5.

p. 2   "Can we wait 500 days? . . ." *Connecticut Post,* January 15, 1997, p. A5.

p. 2   "We should have improved . . ." *New York Times,* October 28, 1996, p. A6.

p. 2   "Our situation is unbearable. . . ." *New York Times,* January 13, 1997, p. A3.

p. 2   "The sense that Bulgaria needed . . ." Pamela Mitova, *Bulgaria: A Country Study* (Washington, D.C.: Library of Congress, 1993), p. 61.

pp. 3–4   "The average European . . ." *New York Times,* Travel Section, June 23, 1996, p. 17.

p. 4   "It's a question of where we are . . ." *New York Times,* April 28, 1995, p. A11.

p. 6   "We Bulgarians are such people . . ." Alison Smale, "Bulgarians Fearful of Future," Associated Press News Service, July 21, 1996. CD NewsBank.

p. 6   "Work left for later . . ." Kirilka Stavreva, *Bulgaria* (New York: Marshall Cavendish, 1997), p. 47.

2

In the Powder Keg of Europe

(Prehistory to 1919)

*F*ew lands in Europe have been inhabited longer than Bulgaria. Archaeologists have found evidence of cave dwellers living in parts of the country as far back as perhaps 100,000 years ago. In all that time, the people of this rugged land have known little peace. Bulgaria's history, like that of its neighbors on the Balkan Peninsula, is riddled with bloodshed, violence, and war that has often spread across the continent. It has earned the region the title the "Powder Keg of Europe."

Early Civilizations and Their Downfalls

The first people to establish a civilization in Bulgaria were the Thracians. They arrived from the north during the Bronze Age around 4000 B.C. The empire they established, called Thrace, included not only present-day Bulgaria but most of the Balkan Peninsula and Romania.

The Greek historian Herodotus described the Thracians as "the most numerous of peoples after the Indians [people of India]," and that "only their chronic disunity prevents them from being the most powerful of all nations." The Thracians were, in fact, a people of curious contrasts. They loved music, literature, and philosophy. They also loved war and killed and looted their neighbors with a savage ferocity. Yet they seemed to have gotten along with the Greeks, their neighbors to the south, and allowed them to build trading centers along their coastline on the Black Sea.

The Macedonians, under the strong leadership of Philip II (382–336 B.C.), conquered Thrace in the fourth century B.C. Philip's son, Alexander the Great (356–323 B.C.), ruled the Thracians until his early death, when the empire he had built crumbled. Within the next two centuries the Romans invaded Thrace and made it a part of their vast empire. The Thracians were subjugated by the Romans, and many of them were enslaved. Their civilization vanished into the mists of history, but the name Thrace remained on the map of Europe into the 20th century as a geographic section of the Balkans.

In A.D. 330 the Roman emperor Constantine the Great (c.288–337) moved his capital from Rome to Byzantium, one of the cities that the Thracians let the Greeks establish on the Bosporus Strait, which connects the Black Sea and the Sea of Marmara. The city's name was changed to Constantinople in the emperor's honor. In 395 the Roman Empire split in two with the West Roman Empire still centered in Rome and the East Roman Empire in Constantinople. The western empire went into decline, its collapse hastened by barbarian invasions from the north, but the eastern empire, known as the Byzantine Empire, expanded and flourished.

While these events were taking place, two new peoples moved into what is now Bulgaria. The Slavs were a peaceful, farming people who came from southern Poland and Russia in the sixth century. Less than a century later, their peace was threatened by fierce warriors called Bulgars (BOOL-gars) who thundered across the plains of Central Asia on horseback. The word Bulgar comes from an Old Turkic word that means "one of mixed nationality." As fierce as they were, the Bulgars were no match for the more civilized Slavs, and they gradually became assimilated into Slavic culture. Out of this commingling of the two groups a new people were born—the Bulgarians.

The First and Second Bulgarian Kingdoms

Bulgar aggressiveness and Slavic order helped the Bulgarians form a new civilization of their own. In 681 Bulgar Khan (HAN), or Prince, Asparuhk (as-pa-ROOHK) (reigned 680–701) broke with the Byzantine Empire, which had previously dominated his people, and established the First Bulgarian Kingdom. Over the next two centuries the kingdom stretched from Macedonia in the north to Albania and Serbia in the west and parts of the Byzantine Empire in the east. It reached its apex under the wise and firm rule of Simeon I (see boxed biography), who came to power in 893 and gave himself the title of czar, a Slavic version of "Caesar." Simeon ushered in a golden age of art, literature, and trade.

The kingdom, however, was short-lived. By 1018 the larger Byzantine Empire swallowed up the Bulgarian Kingdom after a series of debilitating wars. Internal conflicts and new barbarian invasions weakened the empire. By 1186 the Bulgarians were able to break free again and establish the Second Bulgarian Kingdom under Ivan I. The kingdom grew and prospered under Ivan's son Czar Kaloyan (ka-lo-YAN) and his grandson

Over the centuries, Bulgaria has been invaded and conquered many times. This illustration from a medieval chronicle depicts an early Russian invasion.
(The New York Public Library Picture Collection)

Simeon I

(c.863–927, reigned 893–927)

If Bulgaria ever had a "golden age," it was surely under the rule of Simeon I, considered one of his country's greatest monarchs. Warrior lord, patron of the arts, and religious leader, Simeon was a superb national leader in every way.

Christianity, although a relatively new religion in Bulgaria, ran deep in his blood. His father Boris I (reigned 852–889) gave up his throne to become a monk, only to see his eldest son Vladimir (vla-di-MIR) turn his back on the church and attempt to revive Bulgaria's pagan gods. Boris returned from his monastery, deposed Vladimir, and made his younger son, Simeon, king.

Simeon quickly proved himself a strong leader. He went to war against his country's main rival in the region, the Byzantine Empire, defeated it soundly, and came close to taking its capital, Constantinople. He conquered Serbia and vanquished the dreaded warrior tribe the Magyars, driving them into present-day Hungary.

Simeon embraced the Eastern Orthodox Church,[*] rather than the Roman Catholic Church, determining the religious path of his people for the next two millennia. He established a national church, the Bulgarian Orthodox Church, and made the archbishop of Bulgaria a patriarch, the highest ranking bishop in this new church. This church remains the largest religious group in Bulgaria to this day.

A dedicated scholar, Simeon encouraged and supported the translation of Greek literature into the Slavonic language of the church. The arts, especially literature, reached new heights during his reign.

In 925, two years before his death, Simeon named himself czar of all the Bulgars and autocrat of the Greeks. The First Bulgarian Kingdom, however, did not survive him by long. His son and successor, Peter, did not have his strengths and the empire quickly fell apart under the weight of foreign and internal turmoil.

---

[*]The eastern and western Christian churches split in 1054, after drifting apart for several centuries. The Eastern Orthodox Church was a federation of churches united by common beliefs but independent in each nation or region. The Roman Catholic church was united under the authority of the pope in Rome.

Ivan II (reigned 1218–41), who came to control all of the Balkan peninsula, except for Greece.

Bulgarian culture and influence reached its second high watermark in the 13th century. Many centuries would pass before the Bulgarians would again enjoy such freedom and happiness.

In the Grip of the Ottoman Turks

By the early 1300s, a new conqueror was coming out of central Asia into the Middle East. The Ottoman Turks were fierce nomadic warriors, who also had a genius for governing the peoples they conquered. From their Middle Eastern base they moved westward into Christian Europe. They gradually conquered the Byzantine Empire and the regions surrounding it, including the Balkans. By the end of the century they had taken over all of Bulgaria. In 1453 the Turks broke the Byzantine stronghold at Constantinople and made the city the headquarters of their growing empire. Today this city is known as Istanbul. Ottoman supremacy in Bulgaria was unchallenged and would remain so for the next 500 years.

Thousands of Turks poured into Bulgaria and brought with them their government, culture, and Muslim religion. By the end of the 16th century, two-thirds of the population of Sofia, the capital, was Turkish.

The Bulgarians who were willing to convert to the Muslim religion were dealt with fairly, even kindly by the Turks. Those that refused to give up Christianity and their national identity were dealt with harshly. When met by resistance, the Turks were merciless. Entire villages and towns who fought back were wiped out. Land and property of local farmers were seized. Heavy taxes were imposed on the populace. The Bulgarians countered with a series of revolts—in the 1590s, the 1680s, and the 1730s. Each rebellion was crushed by the Turks, but a national movement for independence took root and grew.

One of the leaders of the cause of Bulgarian nationalism was a monk, Father Paisiy (pa-I-si) (1722–73), who lived in the monastery of Hilendar on Mount Athos in Macedonia. In 1762 he wrote the first literary work in

The outcome of the Russo-Turkish War ended 500 years of Turkish rule in Bulgaria. However, many Bulgarians suffered in the conflict before independence. Here, Turkish infantry is shown storming the village of Kizila, which is consumed by flames. (The New York Public Library Picture Collection)

the modern Bulgarian language, *History of Slavo-Bulgarians*. It would circulate among the populace for nearly a hundred years in manuscript form before being published, fueling the fires of patriotism.

As the Turkish state was weakened by numerous wars with its enemies, more freedom was granted to the Bulgarians to keep them content and less rebellious. Local schools teaching in the Bulgarian language opened, the Bulgarian Orthodox Church was revived, and new printing presses published Bulgarian books and newspapers.

But these social reforms only whetted the people's appetite for political autonomy. In April 1876 they staged what would be their last uprising against the Turks. Bulgarian farmers fought the well-armed Turkish army with crude homemade weapons. They fashioned cannons out of cherry trees lined with copper from the pipes of vats used to distill rose oil.

The uprising failed and this time Turkish reprisals were extreme. They destroyed some 100 villages and five monasteries. An estimated 30,000 people—men, women, and children—were massacred in what the international press darkly referred to as "the Bulgarian atrocities."

Januarius MacGahan (1844–78), an American war correspondent for the London *Daily News,* wrote this sobering account on entering the Bulgarian village of Batak (ba-TAK) after the Turks had finished with it:

> I could distinguish one slight skeletal form still enclosed in a chemise, the skull wrapped with a colored handkerchief, and the bony ankles encased in the embroidered footless stockings worn by Bulgarian girls. The ground was strewn with bones in every direction, where the dogs had carried them off to gnaw them at their leisure. At the distance of a hundred yards beneath us lay the town. As seen from our standpoint, it reminded one of the ruins of Herculaneum or Pompeii.

Independence—Of a Sort

Such scenes of slaughter shocked the world and sealed the fate of a decaying, tyrannical empire. Imperial Russia, anxious to expand its own sphere of influence, used the repression of the Balkan Slavs as an excuse to go to war against the Turks. During the Russo-Turkish War (1877–1878), Russian troops marched in and enlisted Bulgarian patriots to fight with them. At the famed battle at the Shipka Pass the Russians and Bulgarians were hopelessly outnumbered by Turkish troops, but they nonetheless took the day. Some 13,000 Turks died in the fighting, but only 5,500 Russians perished. After five centuries of Turkish rule, Bulgaria was liberated.

It was a historic moment that the Bulgarian people would never forget. The bond forged between Russians and Bulgarians at the Shipka Pass would survive two world wars and 40 years of Soviet domination.

The Treaty of San Stefano in 1878 established Bulgaria as an autonomous republic within the Ottoman Empire, or what was left of it. But the major nations of western Europe had no intention of giving Russia a foothold in the Balkans. At a congress held in Berlin, Germany, later that year, the treaty was seriously revised and territory designated to be returned to Bulgaria was taken back, including Macedonia, which remained under Turkish rule. Bulgaria itself was divided into three parts, making national unity all but impossible. It was a bitter disappointment for the Bulgarians, the first of many they would experience in the coming years.

The Balkan Wars and World War I

A German prince, Ferdinand (1861–1948), was chosen to govern the country and was crowned its monarch in 1908. One of his first acts as czar was to declare Bulgaria fully independent from the Turks. But Bulgaria was rapidly changing in the decades leading up to this moment. Under Ferdinand, this previously backward agricultural country had its first taste of industrialization. Between 1887 and 1911 the number of industrial plants in Bulgaria rose from 36 to 345. Bulgaria was slowly preparing to enter the 20th century.

Although the Ottoman Empire was "the Sick Man of Europe," according to the Western press, it was still a threat to change in the Balkans. In 1912, Bulgaria joined Greece, Serbia, and Montenegro* in a war to drive the Turks once and for all from European soil. The war was short and ended in utter defeat for the Turks, although they retained Constantinople for a time. The Bulgarians were rewarded with Thrace as a spoil of war, but were denied Macedonia by their allies. They promptly and heedlessly declared war on Serbia, hoping to take Macedonia back by force.

In this Second Balkan War (1913), Bulgaria was hopelessly outnumbered. Greece, Romania, and Montenegro took the side of the Serbs. After less than a month of bloody fighting, the Bulgarians asked for a truce. In the Treaty of Bucharest, Bulgaria lost almost every inch of territory it had gained from the First Balkan War. Macedonia was divided up among the victors, with only a small corner going to Bulgaria.

Serbia was now the dominant country in the Balkans and it wanted back the territories of Bosnia and Herzegovina, which were in the hands of the Austria-Hungarian Empire. When Archduke Francis Ferdinand, heir to the Austro-Hungarian throne, visited Bosnia in June 1914, he

---

*Serbia and Montenegro would both later become part of Yugoslavia.

was assassinated by a Serb nationalist. Soon after, Austria-Hungary, backed by Germany, declared war on Serbia. Russia came to the aid of the Serbs, and World War I was under way.

At first, Bulgaria remained neutral, but in 1915 it sided with Germany and Austria-Hungary. The only other Balkan country to do so was Turkey. King Ferdinand's government hoped to regain its lost territory from the Serbs. The war was a devastating one for the Balkans, and the Bulgarian people protested against their country's participation. The Social Democratic Party, composed of Communists, supported this stance and gained valuable support from the people.

On September 28, 1918, Bulgaria surrendered and signed an armistice with the Allies—principally Great Britain, France, and the United States. When news of this reached Germany one official said, "The war will end in four months, it cannot continue longer because the states will collapse." It ended in German defeat sooner than that. Bulgaria, under the Treaty of Neuilly, was forced to pay reparations to Serbia and its allies. It also lost more territory, this time to the newly formed nation of Yugoslavia, while Greece gained Bulgaria's outlet to the Aegean Sea.

In three wars in just over four years the Bulgarians had lost valuable territory, many lives, and all self-respect. The war-torn country was fraught with political turmoil and unrest. Terrorist groups struggled for control of the country. Many feared the government would break down completely and that anarchy would take over. But another devastating war would take its toll before Bulgaria would find a new kind of stability and peace under the heel of still another conqueror.

NOTES

p. 11   "the most numerous of peoples . . ." R. F. Hoddinott, *The Thracians* (New York: Thames and Hudson, 1981), p. 14.

p. 16   "I could distinguish one slight skeletal form . . ." Dale L. Walker, *Januarius MacGahan: The Life and Campaigns of an American War Correspondent* (Athens, Ohio: Ohio University Press, 1988), p. 178.

p. 18   "The war will end . . ." John Tolland, *No Man's Land: 1918—The Last Year of the Great War* (New York: Doubleday, 1980), p. 449.

3

Terrorism, War, and Stability at a Price

(1919 to 1985)

The end of World War I left Bulgaria in total disarray, both politically and economically. But there was hope for a new and better future. Out of the quagmire of quarreling political parties emerged the Bulgarian Agrarian National Union (BANU), which gained 28 percent of the vote in elections held in 1919. Once in power, the agrarians and their leader, Alexander Stambuliski (Stam-boo-LI-ski) (1879–1923), tried to reform the age-old landholding system and share the land and its wealth with the peasants. Stambuliski ended all attempts to regain lost territory that had led Bulgaria into three devastating wars and focused instead on domestic problems. He made secondary schooling compulsory for all Bulgarian children and supported a new progressive income tax.

Unfortunately, his policies made him as many enemies as friends. Urban workers felt neglected by the agrarians because they favored the peasant farmers and large numbers of them joined the Communist Party. At the same time, Macedonian nationalists were angry with the government for abandoning the fight to regain their ancestral lands.

In 1923, Stambuliski's opponents staged a bloody coup. He was assassinated and his government overthrown. The new government, largely in the hands of the military, was right wing and extremely repressive. In 1924 it outlawed the Communist Party. In retaliation, the Soviet Union sent agents to Bulgaria to engage in acts of terrorism. One of the most brutal of these was the bombing of Sofia's Sveta Nedelia (Sve-TA ne-DE-lya) Cathedral in a plot to kill Czar Boris III (1894–1943). The czar was unharmed in the blast, but more than 100 others died.

A new, more tolerant leader, Andrei Liapchev (an-DREI LYAP-chev), brought some stability to Bulgaria in the late 1920s. But before the country could benefit from his policies, the world economic depression reached eastern Europe. In a short time, 200,000 workers were unemployed and the per capita income of the peasants dropped 50 percent.

In eastern Europe, fascism was on the rise, feeding off the frustrations of downtrodden peoples who wanted economic security and a sense of national self-respect. Liapchev was defeated in the election of 1931 and Zveno (zve-NO), a new political coalition that had the backing of fascist Italy, came to prominence. In 1934, Zveno seized the government in another coup.

Czar Boris Takes Over

Boris III felt the Zveno government would only bring more ruin to Bulgaria and in 1935 he asserted his considerable power and created a royal dictatorship. Boris's authoritarian rule was no worse and probably better than that of any other faction in Bulgaria and brought a much-needed stability to the troubled nation. But it also weakened the country politically. When elections were held in 1938, Boris declared that only individuals without party affiliations could run for office.

But if the czar could control events within his country, the world outside would not be so manageable. Nazi Germany saw Bulgaria as a key to the Balkans, and it began to exert its influence in the country economically by becoming one of its main trade partners.

As the world teetered on the brink of another major war, Boris struggled to remain neutral, but Germany and Italy, the Axis Powers, would not allow him to do so. Germany's promise of regained territory reawakened old nationalistic dreams and the government clamored for an alliance. In March 1941, Bulgaria signed the Tripartite Pact with both Germany and Italy. The die was cast.

A Reluctant Ally

Despite its status as an ally, Bulgaria sent no soldiers to fight for the Axis Powers. Instead, the Germans used Bulgaria as their base of operations in fighting neighboring Greece and Yugoslavia, both of whom supported the Western Allies—the United States and Britain.

While Boris agreed to declare war on the Allies, he refused to break off diplomatic relations with the Soviet Union, which sided with the Allies after the Germans attacked it in 1941. Boris feared his own people would turn on him if they were forced to fight the country that was still seen by many Bulgarians as a liberator and friend.

There was another issue on which Bulgarians would not be coerced into action. Nazi leader Adolf Hitler declared that all Jews in eastern Europe were to be detained and then sent to concentration camps. Boris and his government agreed to pass the anti-Semitic laws the Nazis foisted on them, but they were not prepared to act on them. Bulgaria's 50,000 Jews had lived there for centuries, as they had in many parts of eastern Europe. The Bulgarian people were not willing to have their friends and neighbors sent to an almost certain death. Politicians, religious leaders of the Bulgarian Orthodox Church, intellectuals, and members of the business community joined together to protest the

Boris III stands tall in his military uniform. His royal dictatorship in the 1930s brought stability but politically weakened his country. When the Germans forced an alliance with Bulgaria in World War II, Boris did his best to keep his people out of the fighting and helped spare the lives of thousands of Bulgarian Jews. (Underwood and Underwood/Corbis-Bettmann)

*After the Germans were driven out in World War II, the Soviet Communists
moved in. The only crime these "traitors" being paraded before the people of
Sofia in August 1946 may have been guilty of was resisting the Soviet takeover.*
(UPI/Corbis-Bettmann)

deportation of Jews. Mass demonstrations ensued and soon after the
Bulgarian parliament revoked the anti-Semitic laws. Not one Bulgarian
Jew went to a gas chamber during World War II, a record unmatched by
any other country in Europe.

But Bulgaria did not escape from the war unscathed. The Allied Air
Command heavily bombed the German-occupied country. By the war's
end, 32,000 Bulgarians had lost their lives in the fighting.

In 1943, Czar Boris, who had done his best to cushion his people from
the ravages of the war, died mysteriously shortly after visiting Hitler in
Berlin. To this day there is speculation that he was secretly murdered by
either Hitler or Soviet agents. His successor was his six-year-old son,
Simeon II (see boxed biography, chapter 5). As the fortunes of war were
shifting in the Allies' favor, Bulgaria tried to make peace with the United
States and Britain. But in September 1944, during peace talks with these

countries, the Soviet Union declared war on Bulgaria. Within days, Soviet troops overran the country.

The Soviet Union's Little Brother

At first the Communists seemed willing to share power with the other political parties in Bulgaria in a coalition called the Fatherland Front. But over the next two years they gradually took control of the front and won over half the seats in the National Assembly in elections held in the fall of 1946. Georgi Dimitrov (ge-OR-gi di-mi-TROF) (1882–1949), a Communist trained by Russian leader Joseph Stalin, became prime minister in the new government. Those who opposed the Communist government were arrested, put on trial, convicted, and either executed or sent to prison.

The Communists set out to totally eradicate the Agrarian Union, their most serious rival for power. Agrarian leader Nikola Petkov (ni-KO-la pet-KOF) received support and encouragement from the United States to compete politically with the Communists. Yet no sooner was a peace treaty between the United States and Bulgaria ratified in June 1947 than Petkov was arrested on the floor of the Bulgaria parliament. He was tried, convicted, and hanged in September. There would be no further serious resistance to communism in Bulgaria for the next four decades.

In his book *Eastern Europe in the Postwar World,* author Thomas Simons refers to postwar Bulgaria as "a land of small farms and fanatical Communists." There are reasons that explain this fanaticism.

Historically, the Bulgarians looked on Russia and the Soviet Union as a friend and liberator, a view other countries did not share. "Not all that many years have passed since the battlefields of Bulgaria were littered with the bones of Russian warriors who died winning Bulgaria's independence from the Turks," wrote Soviet premier Nikita Khrushchev in his 1970 autobiography.

Besides this, Soviet domination and the stability it brought did not seem so terrible, even to a freedom-loving citizenry. War had been a constant companion for decades. When not at war with their neighbors over territory, the Bulgarians were at war with themselves—nationalist against liberal, Communist against democrat. If nothing else, the Soviets provided stability and security for a populace that had known little of either. They built factories and industrial works in the newly expanding cities that gave jobs to a new class of urban workers, who no longer had to scratch a meager living from the soil on small farms. Those Bulgarians who stayed on the farms now worked on large cooperative farms that used modern machinery, which greatly increased productivity. Both workers and farmers achieved a higher standard of living than they had ever known before.

For all these reasons, Bulgaria soon became Russia's most loyal satellite in the Communist bloc. There would be no Hungarian uprising, no Prague Spring, no Polish Solidarity movement in Bulgaria to challenge Soviet authority as in these other Eastern European countries. Dissent and demonstrations would be all but nonexistent there. Whatever frustrations

Bulgaria's Communist leaders stand secure in their power as they view a parade marking the fourth anniversary of Nazi liberation in 1948. Prime Minister Georgi Dimitrov (fifth from left) would be dead within a year and replaced by Vulko Chervenkov, whose cruelty and devotion to the Soviet Union would earn him the nickname "Litte Stalin." (UPI/Corbis-Bettmann)

and dissatisfactions Bulgarians had against the strict regime they lived under they kept them largely to themselves. For 40 years, Moscow would need not worry about its "little brother," Bulgaria. It had no stauncher ally in the world.

In 1949, Premier Dimitrov died in Moscow while undergoing medical treatment and was replaced by Vulko Chervenkov (VUL-ko cher-VEN-kof), a protégé of Soviet leader Joseph Stalin. Chervenkov's enthusiasm for Soviet communism and his ruthlessness in crushing its enemies knew no bounds. While Dimitrov had destroyed the party's opponents, Chervenkov went about removing all those within the party itself who were a threat to his power. He sent thousands of loyal party members to their deaths following show trials, patterned after the ones that Stalin had conducted in Moscow in the 1930s. Chervenkov effectively ended all relations with the West and created a personality cult around himself that earned him the nickname "Little Stalin."

The Rise of Zhivkov

In 1953, Stalin died and Chervenkov suddenly found his position less secure. The following year at the sixth Party Congress, Todor Zhivkov (TO-dor JIV-kof) (see boxed biography), a long-time party official and World War II partisan leader, was named first secretary of the party's Central Committee. He became the youngest person in the Communist bloc to be so honored. Chervenkov hung on to power for two more years, but in 1956 the rise of Soviet leader Nikita Khrushchev and the rapid progress of de-Stalinization all but assured his downfall. At the April meeting of the Central Committee, Zhivkov publicly attacked Chervenkov and his personality cult and the leader was quickly replaced as premier by Anton Yugov (an-TON YOO-gof).

Zhivkov's consolidation of power was completed when Khrushchev visited Bulgaria in 1962 and gave the younger man his blessing. That same year Chervenkov was expelled from the party and Zhivkov ousted Yugov and made himself premier.

The new Communist leader was as much a pawn of the Soviets as his predecessor had been. He followed Soviet policy slavishly, ordered the Soviet flag flown alongside the Bulgarian one, and declared the anniversary of the Russian Revolution a national holiday. On the other hand,

Zhivkov was modest about his accomplishments, took pride in his ordinariness, and fully played the role of a man of the people. As the years passed, Zhivkov initiated modest economic reforms, liberalized censorship, and gradually opened the door to diplomatic relations and trade with the West.

But he was far from universally loved at home. In 1965, a year after Khrushchev's fall from power, Zhivkov's political enemies attempted a coup, the first such to occur in a Communist-bloc country. The coup failed and Zhivkov was quick to blame it on pro-Chinese elements.[*] More perceptive observers blamed the coup on Zhivkov himself and his rigid adherence to Soviet policy.

When the Soviets cracked down on Czechoslovakia's liberal movement in 1968, named Prague Spring, Zhivkov was quick to send troops to help the Soviets subdue the Czechs, while tightening censorship at home.

In 1971, Zhivkov put forth a new national constitution that solidified the power of the Communist Party while appearing to give the people more freedom. With the aborted coup behind him and secure in his power, Zhivkov felt confident enough to strike a more statesmanlike pose on the world stage. He established diplomatic relations with West Germany and the United States, visited President Charles de Gaulle of France, and improved relations with the Catholic Church in a visit with Pope Paul VI.

To prove he was a true Bulgarian, despite his close ties to Russia, Zhivkov championed his country's cultural heritage. He appointed his daughter Luidmilla head of the state commission on art and culture in 1973. Her efforts in this area reached its culmination in Bulgaria's 1,300th anniversary as a nation in 1981 with a national celebration of the arts. As part of the celebration, Zhivkov gave recognition to the Bulgarian Orthodox Church as a codefender of the nation and lifted some restrictions on public worship.

A Tarnished Reputation

But 1981 was also the year that Bulgaria's international reputation was seriously tarnished. Pope John Paul II was wounded in an assassination

---

[*]The Chinese Communists had broken relations with the Soviets several years earlier.

Todor Zhivkov

(1911–1998)

He was the longest-ruling dictator in the Communist world and his very mediocrity may have been the secret of his success. "The Russians were perfectly satisfied to see their most secure Balkan fortress in the hand of an average man who was fully dependent on their will," wrote historian Nissen Oren. But for all his dependence on the Soviets, Zhivkov managed to do enough good for his country to make him as popular at home for many years as he was in Moscow.

He was born into a family of poor but devout peasants in a village outside of Sofia on September 7, 1911. After completing secondary school in the capital, Zhivkov became a printer in the state printing office, a trade he worked at for the next 12 years. He became involved in the local Communist party and became a full party member in 1932. Little is known of his political activities during the next decade, but he resurfaced as a partisan fighter against the occupying Germans in World War II. When the war ended, Zhivkov was elected to the new National Assembly as a Communist in 1945.

A loyal, if not brilliant, party man and Stalinist, Zhivkov rose through the ranks, becoming a full member of the Politburo, the small, controlling body of the national Communist Party, in 1951. Stalin's death two years later was a watershed in Bulgaria and other satellite countries. With the end of Stalinism, "homebred" Communists such as Zhivkov, were favored over Moscow-trained leaders like Vulko Chervenkov. The rise of Nikita Khrushchev to power in the Soviet Union secured Zhivkov's position in Bulgaria and the two were good friends.

Less formal than Chervenkov, Zhivkov presented himself as a "man of the people" whose humble beginnings and lack of charisma reinforced this public image. His strong allegiance to the Soviets was seen by many Bulgarians as fitting in a country where the Russians were still looked up to as liberators.

Among his achievements in his 33-year reign, were the collectivization of Bulgarian agriculture, so complete that it served as a model for other eastern European countries; the resumption of relations with the West, however tentative; and a rapprochement with religion, culminating in a visit with Pope Paul VI in 1975. On the negative side, his organized persecution of ethnic Turks in the 1980s was a dark stain on Bulgaria's international reputation and further discredited a government suspect for shady dealings with terrorists in the developing nations of the world.

With Communist governments collapsing all around him and a failing economy at home, Zhivkov became the scapegoat of his own party in 1989. He was deposed and put on trial for crimes against the Bulgarian people. Political crimes were difficult to pin on him because of a lack of evidence. But after a trial that lasted 18 months, Zhivkov was convicted of embezzlement of state funds and sentenced to a seven-year prison term. Due to heart problems, he was allowed to serve his time under house arrest. In February 1996 Zhivkov was acquitted of the original charges. He died unrepentant on August 5, 1998 at the age of 86. A dinosaur of the Communist world, Zhivkov had the misfortune to outlive all his patrons and protectors.

The longest-ruling dictator in the Communist world, Todor Zhivkov was near the end of his reign when this picture was taken in 1985 during a state visit to Japan. Despite the big grin, Zhivkov was facing serious problems at home, both economically and politically.
(Reuter/Corbis-Bettmann)

attempt by a Turkish nationalist who claimed the plot had been engineered by Bulgarian and Soviet intelligence agents. Although three Bulgarians accused as coconspirators were acquitted in 1986, Bulgaria's name was added to a U.S. State Department list as a sponsor of terrorism. The United States had other reasons to suspect Bulgaria of assisting terrorists. Bulgaria did little to hide the fact that throughout the 1980s it was supplying arms and military equipment to 36 nations around the world, many of them developing nations with active terrorist organizations.

Then in 1984, Zhivkov began what would be the most damaging campaign of his long regime. Fearing that the high birthrate of Bulgaria's ethnic Turkish population would turn Bulgarians into a minority within their own country, he initiated a drastic policy of forced assimilation. Turks who had been living peacefully in Bulgaria for centuries were told they would have to take Bulgarian names and could not speak Turkish in public. Rather than give up their ethnic identity, many Turks emigrated and returned to Turkey. Hundreds of others were forcibly expelled from Bulgaria, arrested and imprisoned, or even killed by Zhivkov's secret police. A total of over 300,000 Turks left the country and returned to Turkey, creating one of the most massive exoduses in Balkan history. Whole communities in Bulgaria lost valuable workers in factories and businesses, while Turkey could not assimilate so many new immigrants and unemployment rates soared. Zhivkov later retracted his policy and many of the Turk nationals returned, but the damage had been done.

In 1982, Khrushchev's successor, Leonid Brezhnev, died, and Zhivkov found himself without a patron. Yuri Andropov, who replaced Brezhnev, disliked the Bulgarian leader because Zhivkov had not supported him for the position of party leader. Then in 1985, Mikhail Gorbachev took the reins of power in Moscow. Gorbachev was a new kind of Soviet leader—pragmatic, energetic, and anxious to reform the Communist system in order to save it from itself. He made it clear to Bulgaria that it would have to reform itself as well if it wanted the continued support of its big brother. For Todor Zhivkov, the man who had followed the Soviet hard line through good times and bad, this was not encouraging news.

NOTES

p. 24   "a land of small farms . . ." Thomas W. Simons, Jr., *Eastern Europe in the Postwar World*. (New York: St. Martin's Press, 1991), p. 59.

p. 24   "Not all that many years . . ." Nikita S. Khrushchev, *Khrushchev Remembers* (Boston: Little, Brown, 1970), p. 366.

p. 28   "The Russians were perfectly satisfied . . ." *Current Biography Yearbook 1976* (New York: H.W. Wilson Co., 1977), p. 460.

4

The Deepening Quagmire

(1989 to Present)

*I*nterestingly, the mass demonstration that rocked the seemingly un-shakable Communist government of Bulgaria was not set off by economics or politics but environmental issues. In one sense, it was fitting. In 40 years, the Communist regime had transformed the natural beauty of Bulgaria into an environmental nightmare with recklessly unregulated industry and rampant pollution.

In October 1989 an international conference on the environment convened in Sofia. The choice of site must have held rich irony for local environmentalists since Sofia, and the area surrounding it, was, and remains today, one of the most polluted regions in the country. Seizing the opportunity to make the world aware of the corrupt regime that could allow this to happen, the few dissident groups in Bulgaria organized a mass rally in the capital.

Five thousand Bulgarians marched on the National Assembly building on November 3 in what was the largest unofficial demonstration in the country in more than four decades. While the environment drove some to demonstrate, many more people used the issue as an excuse to protest against a government that had polluted nearly every aspect of Bulgarian life—economic, political, and social.

The protestors had chosen their moment wisely. To suppress the demonstration with so many foreigners present for the conference would have been an embarrassment for the government, and it allowed the protest to run its course.

The Fall of Zhivkov

The demonstration sent shock waves through the Communist government, whose leaders had until then felt confident they could avert the fate of similar regimes throughout Eastern Europe. Anxious to nip any discontent in the bud, the younger, moderate wing of the Party, led by Foreign Minister Petar Mladenov (PE-tar me-LA-de-nof), offered the people a scapegoat. Todor Zhivkov, who had ruled Bulgaria for 33 years, was 78 years old, weak, and out of touch with the country he had governed so long. Many people blamed Zhivkov for a depressed economy and such unpopular policies as the anti-Turk campaign in the 1980s. Mladenov and his colleagues in the party hierarchy forced Zhivkov to resign. The announcement was made on November 10, only a week after the historic demonstration in Sofia.

With Zhivkov's fall, wrote Clyde Haberman in the *New York Times*, Bulgaria was no longer "in the rear guard of the Communist world, plodding along amid the rush of events. . . . A new breed of Bulgarian dissidents has begun to speak out to a degree rarely heard in this Slavic nation."

This new breed quickly consolidated its power. As the Communists cleaned house, removing hard-liners from high positions in the party and replacing them with moderates, a group of 16 prodemocratic parties formed a coalition and called themselves the Union of Democratic Forces

Zhelyu Zhelev (1935–)

"**A** good-natured man with good intentions," is how one member of the National Assembly describes former president Zhelyu Zhelev. His good nature did not stop him from challenging the Communist government when it took real courage to do so. But his good intentions have not always made him the most effective leader of his nation in his six years in office.

Zhelev studied philosophy at Sofia University in the 1960s. A brilliant student and independent thinker, he dared to criticize the father of Soviet socialism, Vladimir Lenin, in his doctoral dissertation. Although he got his degree, he was expelled from the Communist Party and was exiled to northern Bulgaria where he lived with his family.

Zhelev soon became his country's most outspoken dissident. In his book *Fascism* he compared communism to the dictatorial governments of such fascist countries as Nazi Germany. The book was quickly banned in Bulgaria, but became an underground best-seller and has since been translated into English.

Zhelev's uncompromising stand against the Communists made him the undisputed leader of the small Bulgarian dissident movement in the 1980s. He led the UDF in its struggle against the state and was almost unanimously chosen to replace Petar Mladenov as president by the new National Assembly in 1990.

His popularity, however, gradually fell as one government after another came and went. Zhelev seemed to coexist too well with the former Communists. While he was never accused of political corruption, he was not perceived as taking a strong enough stand against it. His popularity with the Socialists in their last government, may have sullied his reputation with many Bulgarians.

(UDF). The leader of the UDF was a former Communist and one of Bulgaria's few well-known dissidents, Zhelyu Zhelev (JE-yoo JE-lef) (see boxed biography). Zhelev, a philosopher and writer, had been expelled from the party in 1965 when he openly questioned some of Lenin's[*] theories.

---

[*]V. I. Lenin was one of the leaders of the 1917 Russian Revolution and a major Communist theorist.

When he did take action, it often had mixed results. For example, when Zhelev refused to let the Socialists form a new government after the resignation of Zhan Videnov (jan VI-de-nof) he made a strong statement against the Socialists. But he also left his country to flounder without any government at all.

"The fall of the Socialist Party from power is inevitable, as it has proved unable to lead the country out of the crisis," Zhelev said back in May 1996. Unable himself to lead his country, his own fall from power may also have been inevitable. Perhaps now that he is a private citizen once more, Zhelev will become a more effective spokesperson for a better, more democratic Bulgaria.

A courageous dissident for decades, Zhelyu Zhelev disappointed many of his supporters in his six-year tenure as president by getting along too well with the former Communists.
(Nancy Shia/Impact Visuals)

In January 1990 the Communists agreed to meet for talks with the UDF, while Zhivkov, the longest-ruling leader in the Communist world, was arrested and charged with numerous crimes against the Bulgarian people. He later became the first Communist leader to be sentenced in a court of law. By putting all the blame for Bulgaria's problems on Zhivkov, the Communists hoped to stay in power. But under increasing pressure from the people and UDF leaders, they agreed to the first free and open elections in over 40 years of Communist rule.

*The jubilation of these demonstrators at a November 1989 rally in Sofia at the resig-
nation of Zhivkov would not last long. His replacement, Petar Mladenov, whose picture is held by the woman, would continue Communist policies, until he in turn
was forced to resign less than a year later.* (Reuters/Corbis-Bettmann)

From Communist to Socialist

The government, however, was not in retreat; it was merely regrouping.
In a clever move, the Bulgarian Communist Party changed its name to the
less offensive Bulgarian Socialist Party and prepared for the June elections
of delegates to the National Assembly. Although unpopular, the "Socialists" were still better organized and better known than their new and
inexperienced opponents. As a result, they received 48 percent of all votes
cast and won a majority of seats in the new assembly.

But the struggle was far from over. That summer anti-Communist
students, intellectuals, and other dissidents set up tents in central Sofia in
what they declared to be a "Communist-free zone." Others referred to it
as the "City of Truth."

Petar Mladenov, Zhivkov's successor, was shown on a videotape made back in December 1989 during demonstrations saying: "The best thing to do is to bring in the tanks." A remark that a few years before would have had no impact, now was inflammatory. Thousands cried out for Mladenov to resign as party general secretary and president. He did and was replaced as president by an overwhelming vote in the assembly by Dr. Zhelev, who became the first non-Communist president of Bulgaria since World War II. The presidency, however, was largely a ceremonial office with little real authority.

The Socialists clung stubbornly to power, but their grip was slipping. With democratic governments coming to power in country after country in Eastern Europe, the Bulgarian regime became more and more isolated. A general strike that largely paralyzed the nation rendered the government all but helpless and unable to govern. The Socialists resigned before the end of 1990.

The Failure of Democracy

A coalition government took over, largely led by the UDF, whose members held key positions in the cabinet. The new Republic of Bulgaria (previously the Communist-led People's Republic) adapted a Western style democratic constitution and scheduled new parliamentary elections for October 1991. This time, the UDF was the undisputed winner, with the Socialists running second. Just behind then, was the ethnic Turkish party, the Movement for Rights and Freedoms (MRF), which united with UDF in a new coalition that formed a government in November. This government, led by Prime Minister Filip Dimitrov (FI-lip di-mi-TROF), promised full rights to citizens, a better life under a free market economy, and other reforms, but few of its promises were fulfilled. The Socialists were still a considerable force in the assembly and the machinery of the old Communist Party was still in place. To dismantle the state would be a major undertaking and the democratic government had neither the strength nor the support to accomplish this feat.

Within a year, the people's optimism had turned to skepticism. The UDF had lost the support of the MRF and a number of its own supporters had become dissenters. Its stringent economic policies had turned the

Their faces reflecting a nation's frustration and dismay, these demonstrators discuss their concerns with opposition leader Stoian Ganev (back to camera) in 1991. While the Socialists, former Communists, resigned from power in late 1990, they still dominated the new parliament and would soon return to power. (Leo Ecken/Impact Visuals)

trade union, private businesses, and even the Bulgarian Orthodox Church against it. At the end of 1992 the government resigned after a no-confidence vote from the National Assembly.

Another coalition, anti-Communist government was formed, under Lyuben Berov (LYOO-ben BE-rof), an economics professor. Berov vowed to take industry and big business out of the state's grip and privatize it by allowing private individuals and companies to run it. But the financial mess he inherited from the Dimitrov regime made the task all but impossible. He tried to balance the budget by making deep cuts in health, education, and national defense, which brought sharp criticism from many people. Angry farmers incensed by the slow pace of returning collective farms to individual farmers came to the capital to demonstrate in April 1993.

Besieged from every side, Berov stepped down in September 1994 and President Zhelev appointed a caretaker government to prepare the way for new elections.

What economic reforms Berov had delivered had not been well received by the people. Their everyday lives seemed to get worse, not better. The torturous process of transition from the state-run economy to a free-market one made many Bulgarians long for the stability of the former Communist state. In the fall of 1994 the people voted to return the Bulgarian Socialist Party to power.

A Corrupt Government

The same movement back to former Communist leaders had taken place in Poland, Hungary, and Romania. The difference was in these countries the former Communists were careful to continue democratic policies, albeit more cautiously. In Bulgaria, the "Socialists" had no intention of dismantling the state they had spent 40 years building.

The new prime minister was Zhan Videnov, a 35-year-old Moscow-trained Communist and probably the most dedicated leftist governing in the region. But at first, Western observers saw Videnov and his new breed of communism as a breath of fresh air. "They saw the Videnov technocrats come in, wearing nice suits and speaking English, and said these people will move Bulgaria ahead," said political analyst Evgenii Dainov (ef-GE-ni DAI-nof). "They did nothing of the kind."

Under Videnov, Bulgaria took three steps back from democratic reform. No further movement was made toward privatization of state industry, even after the World Bank offered to give funds, support, and retraining for workers to help ease the transition from a state economy to a free-market one. Western investments were discouraged and several of the biggest foreign investors left the country. Much worse, thousands of young Bulgarians were leaving their homeland to look for better job opportunities abroad.

Videnov's government had the dubious distinction of being the only post-Communist government in Eastern Europe to show no interest in joining the North Atlantic Treaty Organization (NATO).[*] As one foreign diplomat put it: "Bulgaria will not do anything with regards to NATO which it is not totally confident that the Russians approve of and want to

---

[*] An international group of 15 Western nations formed in 1949 to defend themselves collectively against aggression, particularly from the Soviet Bloc.

happen." The Socialist government renewed friendly relations with Russia and was promised increased trade and other useful exchanges from the Russians in return for a renewal of the close ties the two countries enjoyed in the Soviet era.

But national self-interest and ideology were not the only motives for the government's hard-line policies. There was also personal greed. Instead of privatizing state-owned industry, government officials allowed Party members in business to help themselves to literally billions in assets in floundering companies. Then they allowed them to send the money abroad to be stashed away in foreign banks. Within a short time nearly all of Bulgaria's 47 state-owned and private banks were insolvent. The entire country was going bankrupt while a few were growing rich on the misery of the masses. "People's savings were going into a black hole," observed one Western banker. Thousands lined up at banks to remove their savings before it was too late. "I haven't seen a time like this since after the war, when my father had to sell his shoes for bread," complained one elderly woman waiting to withdraw her life's savings. "When I get my money, I'm keeping it at home. I have no confidence in any bank anymore."

Inflation soared, as did the prices of staples like bread. Sofia and other cities were filled with long lines of people waiting to buy a loaf of bread that they could barely afford. Workers' salaries by early 1996 had hit rock bottom—$30 a month, lower than Albania, the poorest country in Europe.

Even law and order, one area that the Communists had prided themselves on, was unraveling. Crime and violence were becoming rampant. The crisis reached a peak on October 2, 1996, when former prime minister Andrei Lukanov (an-DREI loo-KA-nof) who had led two previous Socialist governments in 1989 and 1990, was gunned down in broad daylight by an assassin as he was leaving his home. Rumors spread quickly that Lukanov, who was one of Videnov's sharpest critics, was killed for political reasons. The crime remained unsolved more than a year later.

A New President and Some Hope

Betrayed by the Socialists, who they had entrusted to make life better in a world of chaos and change, the Bulgarian people took their anger to the polls. In late October 1996 the first round of elections for president were held. President Zhelev, who had lost much of his popularity by railing against the Socialist government but doing little to improve the situation, lost his bid for reelection in the primary. Ivan Marazov (i-VAN ma-RA-zof), the Socialist candidate, came in a poor second to UDF candidate Petar Stoyanov (PE-tar sto-YA-nof), who won about 45 percent of the vote. A month later Stoyanov won the final round with over 60 percent of the vote.

Numerous strikes and demonstrations took place across the country as the people voiced their deep displeasure with the Socialist government. Losing his ability to govern at all under the pressure of civil unrest, Prime Minister Videnov finally resigned in late December 1996. Interior Minister Nikolai Dobrev (ni-KO-la DO-bref) was nominated to replace him, but President Zhelev, still in office, refused to allow Dobrev to form a new government.

Bulgaria, already in dire economic straits, entered the new year without a stable government. Basic services were now endangered. Hospitals closed in some cities and in others the doctors, shamefully underpaid, sent home all but the sickest of their patients. Schools, unable to afford to heat classrooms, reduced class periods and sent students home early. Unable to pay for fuel to keep their homes warm, families and many older people scoured the nearest forest for wood to burn. The country was falling apart.

The seething rage of the people boiled over. Tens of thousands took to the streets to protest. On January 10, 1997, they broke into the National Assembly building and went on a rampage. They smashed furniture, destroyed computers, and set fire to an office. For 10 hours they blockaded the entrance and prevented a hundred legislators from leaving the building. The police were called in and with clubs and guns drawn, dispersed the crowd in a bloody melee that left both police and protesters injured. "This is the anger of people who had nothing to lose," said Yordan Sokolov (yor-DAN so-KO-lof), a leading spokesman for the UDF in the assembly.

Order was restored, but the protests continued. Day after day, the streets of Sofia were filled with demonstrators, disrupting traffic and carrying protest signs.

The Socialists' term of office would not expire until 1998, but the people wanted them out much sooner, calling for new elections by May. The Socialists stubbornly refused to resign, promising only to enter into a "wider dialogue" with their political opponents. But a serious division was developing within the Socialist Party itself, with moderates calling for the hard-liners to initiate some reforms and move up the date for elections.

On January 19, Petar Stoyanov was installed as Bulgaria's second democratically elected president. Forty thousand people jammed into Sofia's streets to see the man on whom their frail hopes were now pinned. The 44-year-old lawyer and former soccer star spoke to them of a new tomorrow, of market reforms that would save the plummeting economy, and a new Bulgaria where young and old alike would find a better, brighter future. He also called for new national elections and punishment for corrupt politicians.

". . . in the last four years," Stoyanov said, addressing the crowd, "Bulgaria has seen only an imitation of reforms linked with corruption and arrogant disregard of public opinion. The future of the kids has always been the main concern of every Bulgarian. We have to offer them a society they wish to live in."

After 23 days of public protest, 25,000 students and other dissidents held the largest rally yet in the capital. It was followed by a general strike by the three largest trade unions. Realizing it had to compromise or face greater troubles, the government reluctantly agreed to move up elections to the fall of 1997.

This was not good enough for the people. As protests grew more massive, a transportation strike paralyzed the country. On February 4, President Stoyanov called for an emergency meeting with government leaders. After four hours of intense negotiations, he emerged to announce that the Socialists were stepping down from power and had agreed to hold general elections no later than April 20. The crowd cheered and lifted Stoyanov on their shoulders, carrying him through streets filled with dancing, joyful people.

Stoyanov immediately appointed a caretaker government lead by Sofia mayor Stefan Sofiyanski until the elections could be held. When elections were held in April the UDF won big—137 out of 240 assembly seats. The Socialists took only 58. A new coalition government was formed under the leadership of 48-year-old economist Ivan Kostov (i-VAN KOS-tof) who was elected prime minister.

In its first session held on May 7, 1997, the new assembly pledged to the Bulgarian people that they would work to improve the economy, reduce crime, and bring Bulgaria closer to the European mainstream.

Those are big promises, but with new democratic leadership, perhaps Bulgaria's time of real transition is about to begin. For many, it is long overdue.

NOTES

p. 33   "in the rear guard of the Communist world . . ." Bernard Gwertzman and Michael T. Kauffman, eds., *The Collapse of Communism* (New York: Times Books, 1990), p. 186.

p. 34   "A good-natured man . . ." *New York Times,* January 15, 1997, p. A3.

p. 35   "The fall of the Socialist Party . . ." Veselin Zhelev, "Bulgarians Line Up for Fuel," The Associated Press News Service, May 27, 1996. CD NewsBank.

p. 37   "The best thing to do . . ." James Naughton, *Traveller's Literary Companion: Eastern & Central Europe* (Lincolnwood, Ill.: Passport Books, 1996), p. 289.

p. 39   "They saw the Videnov technocrats come in . . ." Christine Spolar, "Bulgaria Pays Price for Lagging on Market Reforms," *Washington Post,* July 7, 1996, p. A21. CD NewsBank.

pp. 39–40 "Bulgaria will not do anything . . ." *New York Times,* April 28, 1995, p. A11.

p. 40   "People's savings were going . . ." *New York Times,* October 28, 1996, p. A6.

p. 40   "I haven't seen a time like this . . ." *Washington Post,* July 7, 1996, p. A21.

p. 41   "This is the anger . . ." *Connecticut Post,* January 11, 1997, p. A5.

p. 42   ". . . in the last four years . . ." Veselin Toshkov, "Bulgaria's President Sworn In," Associated Press News Service, January 19, 1997. CD NewsBank.

5

Government

*I*n the early months of 1997, the government of the Republic of Bulgaria was in a state of flux. Both democratic and Socialist administrations had failed in their attempts to build a healthy, new nation on the crumbling foundation of the old one. With a new coalition government in power, it is hoped its leaders will have learned from the mistakes of previous administrations and begin to dig the country out of the economic and political quagmire in which it has sunk. The structure of government set up by the revised constitution of 1991 is a strong one. But it needs politicians who are willing to work unselfishly and courageously for the public good to implement it.

The Three Branches of National Government

Many of the political institutions existing in Bulgaria today were conceived under communism, but they had little if any power then to act independently. The National Assembly, the legislative body, was a mere rubber

44

stamp for the reigning Communist Party's Politburo. The courts were another arm of the state with little independence.

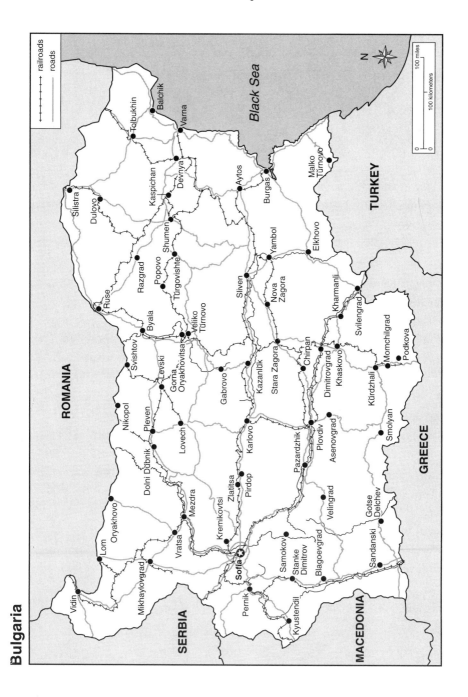

Much of this changed with the collapse of communism and the rise of the first freely elected government in 1990. A new constitution adopted at Veliko Turnovo (ve-LI-ko TUR-no-vo) in July 1991 turned the National Assembly into a truly representative legislative body of 240 members, directly elected by proportional representation. If the National Assembly has been perceived as weak in recent years, it is not because it is powerless. A political stalemate has often resulted from the conflicting interests of representatives of the Bulgarian Socialist Party and the Union of Democratic Forces.

The Republic of Bulgaria has chosen, as have so many of the newly independent Eastern Bloc countries, a parliamentary form of government. The president, while officially the head of state, has far less power than the prime minister, the political leader of the party in power. The president is, however, commander in chief of the armed forces, serves as his country's representative abroad, and can choose the next prime minister with the approval of the National Assembly. He can, as former president Zhelev has done, refuse to name a new prime minister, and create a caretaker government while calling for new elections.

The prime minister, with his cabinet of 17 ministers called the Council of Ministers, runs the government. Each minister is responsible for one facet of government, from finance and foreign affairs to education and the environment.

The president is elected directly by the people and can serve no more than two, five-year terms. The prime minister and his party govern until a crisis leads to a vote of no confidence in the National Assembly and then the government must step down, as the Socialists finally did in early 1997. Then new elections are scheduled to determine the next government.

The judicial branch in many ways has undergone the least changes since 1991. The members of the Supreme court, the highest judicial body in Bulgaria, are elected to five-year terms by the National Assembly. Reform barely touched the court, and judges, until recently, remained one of the poorest paid and least respected professions in the country. In a 1991 poll less than 2 percent of the Bulgarian people trusted in the fairness of the courts. More recent reforms have improved the judicial system, although most people retain their skepticism. There are 105 provincial courts and many more municipal courts that try minor offenses at the local level.

Ex-soccer star and lawyer, President Petar Stoyanov represents the hopes of most Bulgarians for a better, more democratic future. Here he addresses a crowd of over 10,000 supporters shortly before taking office in January 1997. (Agence France Presse/Corbis-Bettmann)

For decades, Bulgaria was politically divided into 28 districts. In 1987 the Communists consolidated these districts into nine provinces, known as *oblasti* (O-bla-sti) (singular *oblast)*. The oblasti are governed locally by the People's Councils, whose members are elected for terms of 30 months. They attend FPto local services, such as police and road repairs.

Political Parties

Until recently, the Bulgarian Socialist Party (BSP) was the largest and most powerful political party in the country. Returning to power in 1994, the Socialists did serious damage to their reputation by hanging on long after they should have stepped down. No longer running the government, the Socialists still remain a force to be reckoned with because of the wealth and political machinery they control.

King Simeon II (1937–)

In 1943, King Boris of Bulgaria died mysteriously and was succeeded by his six-year-old son, Simeon II. Unlike his namesake, Simeon I, the child-king's reign was brief. When the Communists took over the country three years later and abolished the monarchy, he was forced to flee with his mother to Egypt. Soon after Simeon settled in Spain, where he grew up in exile, marrying a Spanish aristocrat and becoming a business consultant.

In May 1996 the exiled king returned home at the invitation of Bulgarian intellectuals, who hoped he would become a leader in post-Communist Bulgaria and help restore order to a troubled land. It was the first time Simeon had stepped on Bulgarian soil in nearly 50 years, and he was greeted warmly by half a million Bulgarians.

While the chance of restoring the monarchy at present seems remote, Simeon's visit sparked hope in many people, starved for stability and tradition. The Socialist government and former president Zhelev were opposed to any kind of monarchy and the new constitution of 1991 banned its return. But in a 1994 survey 22 percent of those Bulgarians asked were in favor of a king. After all they have gone through under the Communists and Socialists, a wise king may have seemed preferable to wily and often corrupt politicians.

A cultured man who is fluent in Spanish, English, French, and German, Simeon is realistic about his chances of becoming a political power in his country. "I'll do what I can, but I do not have the vocation of a spare wheel," he said in an interview in early 1997. "If things go fine without me, then this is a blessing for Bulgaria and for me."

Whether he runs for political office or not, this man who Zheylu Zhelev has called "an important part of Bulgaria's history," could play a positive role in its future.

The Union of Democratic Forces, the other major political party, did not exist before 1990. A true coalition, it was originally made up of 10 organizations who had different beliefs but held several goals in common. They all wanted to see Bulgaria become a country with a constitutional government that provides its citizens with democratic freedoms and a free-market economy. The coalition quickly expanded to include six more groups. Under the leadership of Zhelyu Zhelev, Bulgaria's most visible dissident, the UDF became an effective dissident party against the Communists after the fall of Zhivkov, and later an effective opposition

Simeon II represents stability to many Bulgarians in a world of corrupt politicians. Seen here in 1979 with his Spanish wife, Margarita, he returned to his country for the first time in nearly 50 years in May 1996.
(Reuters/Corbis-Bettmann)

party against the Socialists. There is a great diversity of interests and concerns within the coalition, including such narrowly focused groups as the ecologically minded Green Party. Yet the organization put forth a united front and has proven a sincere dedication to their ideals by twice refusing to form a coalition with the BSP, even though it meant being shut out of government for years.

But more recently there has been division within the UDF itself. In 1991 the largest groups within the coalition fought with the smaller ones who feared they were taking over control of policy making.

Among the smaller political parties in Bulgaria the most interesting and visible is the Movement for Rights and Freedoms. It represents the rights of the Turkish minority in Bulgaria. In the face of deepening anti-Turkish feeling in Bulgaria, the party broadened its stand on civil rights in 1991, when it was the fourth largest party in the country. While denying any call for complete autonomy of Turks within Bulgaria, the MRF has taken a strong stand on the protection of the rights of Turks and other ethnic minorities. It continues to call for the trial of the Communist leaders in the Zhivkov administration responsible for the assimilation campaign against ethnic Turks in the 1980s.

Foreign Policy

For four decades following World War II, Bulgaria's foreign policy was largely built on its close relationship with the Soviet Union. Since the Soviet state collapsed, Bulgaria has looked both east and west to make new friends, while keeping old ones. Close to home, it has attempted to mend relationships with its old enemy Turkey, which has also become a democratic republic. In 1990 and 1991 former president Zhelev met several times with Turkish president Turgot Ozal to increase trade and improve the human rights of ethnic Turks living in Bulgaria. But anti-Turk rhetoric from radical Bulgarian nationalists and bitter Turkish memories of Zhivkov's assimilation campaign make the alliance an uneasy one.

Relations with Russia, the largest of the former Soviet republics, are less uneasy, but not without tension. As Russia has lost much of its influence in such former satellites as Poland, the Czech Republic, and Hungary, it has worked hard to renew its ties with Bulgaria, as well as Romania and Slovakia. While these countries may not need Russia politically, they desperately need its help economically. Promises of military and economic aid kept Bulgarian Socialists firmly within the Russian sphere, although they often spoke about it in cautious terms. On the matter of NATO membership, former deputy foreign minister Vasily Baitchev (va-SI-li BAI-chev) had this to say: "Although we do not consider Russia's position to be decisive, we do believe that Russia's legitimate rights cannot be ignored."

Other Bulgarians felt differently and formed an activist lobby, the Atlantic Club of Bulgaria, to encourage the public to speak out in favor of NATO membership. In February 1997, with the Socialist government weakening and under strong public pressure, the National Assembly voted unanimously to apply for NATO membership. "With its decision, the government responded to the desires of the prevailing majority of the Bulgarian citizens, who feel as an inseparable part of the free world," said president Stoyanov boldly.

With a new coalition government in power, Russia could stand to lose more than it may gain in Bulgaria, although it is unlikely the Bulgarians will try to severe all ties with their former "big brother."

Much of this will depend on Bulgaria's developing relationships with the West. After decades of virtual isolation from Western Europe and the United States, Bulgaria is hoping that renewed relations with the West will bring in some of the investments and aid that has benefited other Eastern European countries such as Poland and the Czech Republic. Former president Zhelev traveled to Europe and the United States in the fall of 1990 to visit with U.S. president George Bush and France's president François Mitterrand, who a year earlier became the first Western head of state to visit Bulgaria since before World War II. Both leaders pledged aid, although far less than what other Eastern European nations have received.

The West is encouraged by Bulgaria's move toward democracy but is watching warily to see if it will avoid the terrible civil chaos that has gone on in the former Yugoslavian lands and, more recently, in Albania. As for Bulgaria, it seems ready to join its neighbors in looking westward.

In August 1997 Bulgarian naval forces joined Turkey, Ukraine, and other Eastern European countries, as well as the United States, in military exercises at a Crimean naval base. It was part of NATO's Partnership for Peace program.

NOTES

p. 48   "I'll do what I can . . . "*New York Times,* January 31, 1997, p. A12.
p. 50   "Although we do not consider . . ." *New York Times,* April 28, 1995, p. A11.
p. 51   "With its decision, the government responded . . . " "Bulgaria Wants to Join NATO," Associated Press News Service, February 17, 1997. CD NewsBank.

6

Religion

Religion has traditionally played a central role in Bulgarian life. The Bulgars adopted Christianity in A.D. 864, becoming one of the first peoples in Eastern Europe to do so. The religious writing of Bulgarian monks and priests were crucial in converting other peoples in Eastern Europe, including the Russians. The Bulgarian Orthodox Church, one of the many nationalistic orthodox faiths in Eastern Europe, was, and remains, fiercely nationalistic. Today, an estimated 86 percent of Bulgarians are members of this church.

The Bulgarian Orthodox Church— Past and Present

Czar Simeon I established the Bulgarian Orthodox Church in the 900s. His palace library was a treasure house of religious learning, and he employed monks to copy precious church manuscripts for posterity. It is said Simeon himself put together a collection of sermons known as *slava* (SLA-va).

When the Bulgarian Empire was swallowed up by the Byzantines, religion again was in the forefront of the resistance. In the 10th century, a Bulgarian priest name Bogomil (BO-go-mil) began a religious movement. The Bogomils, as his disciples were called, were passionately nationalistic, opposed to Byzantine domination and culture, and viewed the material world as the work of the devil. So appealing were the sect's precepts, that they soon spread over much of southern and eastern Europe, taking different names in each country. By the 15th century, Bogomilism was weakened and largely vanquished by the Bulgarian Orthodox Church and the Byzantine Empire, but its ideas were kept alive in Bulgarian folklore and folkways for generations to come.

When the Communists took over Bulgaria after World War II, they recognized that the Bulgarian Orthodox church was closely linked to Bulgarian nationalism and did everything they could to undermine its power and influence. Once a great landholder, the Church was stripped of its property. The legendary Rila Monastery (see boxed feature), was turned into a national museum. While clergy were not banned from practicing, their appointment had to be approved by the state, which also paid their salaries. Church officials and clergymen who did not strictly adhere to the rules laid down by the government were dismissed, imprisoned, or sent into exile. The number of orthodox priests shrunk from 3,312 in 1947, the year after the Communists came to power, to 1,700 in 1985.

When Todor Zhivkov fell from power in 1989 and the Communists began to lose their grip on the country, Bulgaria experienced a religious revival. Church holidays were reinstated. A flurry of baptisms and weddings filled church calendars. Christmas 1990 was a joyous national celebration. An orthodox seminary in Sofia reopened its doors and took in more than 100 students. Rila and other monasteries were returned to a grateful church. Religious expression was something to be celebrated after the long, dark night of communism.

But the Bulgarian Orthodox Church today faces serious problems. Forty years of atheistic Communist rule has left its mark. Whatever nominal church membership they hold, as many as 65 percent of the people don't practice their faith today. There is also a severe shortage of priests, with many older priests facing retirement age. Younger liberal religious leaders are in conflict with their elders, who grew up under the Communist regime and have been accused of collaboration and corruption.

Hopefully this new generation of religious leaders will bring a much needed moral strength and spiritual focus to a church that has too long stood more for nationalism and ritual ceremony than a deep and abiding faith.

The Rila Monastery

The more than 100 medieval monasteries of Bulgaria have been much more than homes for pious monks. For centuries they were centers of learning, repositories of great literature and art, and shining symbols of Slavic civilization when that civilization seemed in danger of disappearing.

Rila is the largest and most celebrated of the Bulgarian monasteries and is one of the oldest in all Europe. It lies 75 miles south of Sofia in the Rila Mountains, a landscape of breathtaking beauty. The monastery was founded in 951 by the holy hermit Ivan Rilski (i-VAN RIL-ski), who has since been canonized as Saint Ivan of Rila.

A stronghold of Bulgarian culture through centuries of oppression under the Byzantines and the Turks, Rila Monastery has suffered every indignity. It has been robbed, burned, and turned into a museum by the Communists. Yet it has survived. Today it has been returned to the Bulgarian Orthodox Church and has been named one of the world's greatest cultural historical sites by the United Nations.

Its painted icons, frescoes, and murals, depicting biblical scenes, still inspire awe, hundreds of years after the gifted monks of Rila created them.

In his poem "Near the Rila Monastery," famed Bulgarian author Ivan Vazov (i-VAN VA-zof) describes the beauty of the surrounding natural landscape, but his words also express what millions of Bulgarians feel about this national treasure:

Now I am truly home—a world it is
Which I adore and seek. Here I breathe freely
And lighter feel; a deep tranquillity
Now fills my breast and waves of new life, sweeping
Into my soul, thrill me with new sensations,
New strength, might and poetic revelations . . .

Bulgarian Jews—A Proud Record

Bulgaria's Jews are mostly descended from Jewish exiles of Spain who fled that country in the 16th century to escape persecution. They settled in Bulgarian cities and were largely assimilated into the population.

Tourists marvel at the ornate paintings that adorn the domed ceilings of the Rila Monastery. The largest monastery in Bulgaria, it is also one of the oldest in all Europe. (Sonja Iskov/ Impact Visuals)

Unlike Jews living in other European countries, Bulgaria's 50,000 Jews were spared the fate of the concentration camps and gas chambers of Nazi Germany, thanks to the compassion and determination of the Bulgarian government and its people. Although an ally of Germany, Bulgaria dragged its feet on the deporting of Jews, knowing they were going to almost certain death. They eventually reversed the anti-Jewish laws the Nazis had foisted upon them early in the war. When the war ended in German defeat, 90 percent of Bulgaria's Jews emigrated to the nation of Israel to start a new life. As of 1990, there were only 6,000 Jews living in Bulgaria. Few of this number practice their faith. There are no rabbis in the country and the few synagogues that remain in Sofia and other cities are only open occasionally.

Other Religions

The second-largest religious group in Bulgaria are Muslims, who make up about 13 percent of the population. They are mostly ethnic Turks who have lived in Bulgaria for centuries, but they also include Pomaks, Gypsies, and Tartars. The vast majority of Muslims live in the northeast and the Rhodope Mountains region.

Of all religious groups, the Muslims probably suffered the most under communism. Persecuted by both the Communists and the Bulgarian Orthodox Church, whose national pride was repulsed by the religion of the Ottoman Empire, the Muslims have enjoyed their own rebirth under a new constitution that upholds religious freedom for all Bulgarian citizens.

Today there are over 1,200 mosques in the country. The largest, the Tumbul Mosque in Shumen (SHOO-men), which also boasts a theological Muslim school, dates back to 1744.

Roman Catholicism has had to struggle for centuries to be accepted in Bulgaria, where the Bulgarian Orthodox Church has traditionally been strongly opposed to its influence. The Communists viewed the Catholic Church with great suspicion and considered it a pernicious "foreign" influence in the country. Sixty Roman Catholic priests were convicted as Western spies in the infamous "Catholic trials" of the early 1950s; four of them were executed. Relations with the Vatican, first started in 1925, were reinstated in 1990 after the fall of communism. In 1991 there were 44,000 Roman Catholics in Bulgaria, mostly living in the cities of Sofia, Plovdiv (PLOV-dif), and Ruse (ROO-se).

Much smaller in number, but quickly growing, are the followers of Protestant denominations. The first missionaries, mostly Methodist and Congregational, arrived in Bulgaria from the United States in 1857. In 1871 the first translation of the complete Bible into Bulgarian was produced by the Union of Evangelical Churches. In more recent years the more charismatic denominations have gained converts. The Pentecostals are the largest Protestant group in Bulgaria today with 5,000 to 6,000 members.

A Land of Superstitions

Centuries of Christianity have not completely eradicated Bulgaria's distant pagan past, and superstitions are still taken seriously, especially by country folk. The same good Christians who attend church on Sunday will wear charms to ward off the evil eye when night falls.

Soothsayers and fortune-tellers still hold as much authority for some Bulgarians as the local priest. The most famous of soothsayers was Vargelia Gushterova (var-GE-li-a GOO-shte-ro-va), popularly known as Aunt Vanga, whose death at age 89 in August 1996 was an occasion for national mourning. Blinded in a windstorm at age 12, Aunt Vanga began to have visions of past and future events, many of them with uncanny accuracy. Her humble home in the village of Rupite (ROO-pi-te), south of Sofia, was a shrine to thousands of Bulgarians who often traveled great distances to consult her. Everyone from Communist leader Todor Zhivkov to current president Petar Stoyanov visited her before making critical decisions. Terminally ill with breast cancer, Aunt Vanga refused to be operated on, and continued to see Bulgaria's sick and troubled people until shortly before her death. "She lived not for herself but for the people," said former prime minister Zhan Videnov. "That made her a living saint for us."

As Bulgaria struggles to free itself from economic disaster and the shackles of Communist ideology in the 21st century, religion will continue to be a force of both faith and hope. Whether it will regain its former glory in a new Bulgaria, however, remains to be seen.

NOTES

p. 54   "Now am I truly home . . ." Naughton, p. 320.

p. 57   "She lived not for herself . . ." *San Diego Union-Tribune*, August 12, 1996, p. B4.

7

The Economy

An impatient Bulgarian taxi driver waiting in a long line for gasoline, the latest shortage in a country where nearly every necessity is in short supply, was heard to complain: "First the bread, now the gas. . . . What's next? Only the dollar is up in this country. Everything else is down."

Bulgaria's economy is indeed down. After years of corruption and chaos one wonders if it can sink any lower. By mid-1996 the national economy stood at $12 billion, three-quarters of what it was in 1989. Most banks were insolvent. Inflation was at an all-time high. Foreign debt stood at $9.4 billion. More than 70 percent of the population was living at or below the poverty line.

Even the once financially secure middle class was struggling to survive. "We buy only food," said Petar Beron (PE-tar be-RON), a museum curator. "I pay some electricity and heating. Clothes are a thing of the past. It is theoretically impossible to make ends meet in these conditions. You might as well go straight to your funeral. But even to die is not so cheap anymore."

It didn't have to be this way. The Bulgarian people made a critical choice in 1994. Discouraged by hardships intensified by privatization and the reforms necessary to turn the planned market economy of the Communists into a free, open-market economy, the people looked to the same Communists, now called Socialists, they had turned out only a few years before to restore stability. But instead of getting better, things only got worse. The Socialists, filled with confidence by their triumphant return to power, stuck to a hard line on the economy. Unlike former Communists in other countries like Poland and Hungary, they remained rigidly ideological and showed none of the political pragmatism that kept reform moving forward elsewhere.

While Prime Minister Zhan Videnov talked about economic reform, his efforts were halfhearted at best. At one point, the mass privatization of industry was to be achieved by selling vouchers to individual citizens in over a thousand state-owned companies, making them small investors in these companies. It sounded good on paper, but in practice little changed.

Half a year after the Socialists took over the government, 90 percent of all state-owned businesses were still run by the state. Many of these companies were inefficiently run and losing money. One computer-disc manufacturer in Pazardzhik (PA-zar-djik) had accumulated $11 million in debt since 1982. But few, from the plant manager to the workers, believed it would close. "We were supposed to be part of the privatization program; now we're going the other way," admitted Felix Domyanov (FE-lix do-MYA-nof), the plant's financial director. "Are they [the government] being honest or not? I've asked myself the same question."

Meanwhile Videnov refused overtures to work with the World Bank and other international institutions to alleviate the country's massive overseas debts. Given a cold shoulder by the government, dozens of Western businesses and investors left the country, followed by tens of thousands of young Bulgarians who could find no job opportunities at home.

It was the economic crisis, more than anything, that led to the downfall of the Socialist government. One only hopes the politicians who have succeeded them will have learned from their mistakes.

Before looking at what efforts are being made to solve the problems of the Bulgarian economy (see chapter 11), let's examine what role industry, agriculture, and natural resources have played in that economy in the past and the present.

Industry

When the Communists took over Bulgaria in the late 1940s, heavy industry barely existed there. While some light industry flourished, especially textile manufacturing and food processing, 80 percent of the people made their living off the land. It was often a miserable living at best, with small farmers using farming techniques that had changed little since the Middle Ages.

The Communists built factories and industrial plants, creating new heavy industry, often at the expense of light industry. By the late 1980s half of Bulgaria's net material product (NMP) came from industry in which one-third of the nation's workers were employed.

The state ran nearly all businesses and while everyone who wanted a job had one, management was poor and operations were wasteful. However, as long as the Soviets helped to keep the Bulgarian economy afloat, the people were generally content. As bad as things might be, their standard of living was generally better than it had been before. But as communism weakened in the 1980s and the Soviet Union's economy began to flounder, it had a ripple effect in Bulgaria. The Soviet Union had its own problems to deal with and Bulgaria was ill equipped to build a strong economy independent of its "Big Brother."

With the collapse of the Communist government, new leaders, looking to Western reforms, began the difficult transition toward a market economy. But the slowness of reform and the "shock therapy" of withdrawing state subsidies that people previously relied on, quickly soured the public to the new leadership. The former Communists who returned to power were no better at improving the situation. "We haven't had a Leszek Balcerowicz or a Vaclav Klaus [two astute economic architects in Poland and the Czech Republic]," laments one worker. "In Bulgaria, we have only the firm hand of Zhan Videnov—and we see where that is leading us."

Traditionally the Soviets encouraged heavy industry—the manufacture of machines, trucks, ships, and tools. To diversify and make Bulgaria less reliant on other countries for consumer goods, the early post-Communist governments supported lighter industry, new technology such as electronics and biotechnology, and foreign investment, especially from the West. The Socialists halted most of these efforts and it can only be hoped the new government will restart the process of serious economic reform.

Agriculture and Natural Resources

More than half of Bulgaria is farmland, and it produces a rich array of crops. In the last years of communism, about a fourth of workers were employed in agriculture, providing a fifth of the country's net material product. Just as industry remained stuck in the state's grip in 1996, transferral of the 90 percent of state-run farmland to private farmers has progressed painfully slowly. In 1993, however, there were more than 1,300 private farms in the country. The farmers who run them are largely free to determine how they will farm, what they will grow, and to whom they will sell their produce.

There are two main agricultural regions in Bulgaria. The first is in the north on the Danubian Plateau. Here are grown wheat, Bulgaria's most important cash crop, other grains, sugar beets, potatoes, and sunflowers. Sunflower seeds are fed to livestock, as are the tall stalks that make excellent fodder. The seeds are also crushed for oil used in cooking or are roasted and eaten by people as a snack. The growing season on the plateau is long enough to also raise apples, pears, and other fruits.

The second agricultural region is the Maritsa (ma-RI-tsa) River Valley in the south where the more temperate conditions allow farmers to raise

Tobacco is one of Bulgaria's biggest crops. These women in the village of Kocherinovo are stringing tobacco leaves to dry. After several weeks, they will sell them for 75 cents a pound to a middleman. He will then sell them to a tobacco factory for processing. (Dick Doughty/Impact Visuals)

The Valley of Roses

"A rose by any other name would smell as sweet," playwright William Shakespeare wrote. But few roses in the world are as prized for their fragrance as those that have been grown in central Bulgaria's Kazanluk (ka-zan-LOOK) Valley, better known as the "Valley of Roses."

One variety of rose, the pink Damask, is grown not for its blossoms, but for the oil that it contains. This oil, known as *attar,* is what gives the flower its fragrance. Attar of rose can be extracted from the blossoms and is a vital ingredient in fine perfumes, cosmetics, soaps, and medicines used to treat patients with respiratory diseases.

Bulgarian attar is the most prized by perfume makers for its uniquely pungent and long-lasting fragrance. The Valley of Roses alone produces about 75 percent of the world's total production of attar. Obtaining the rose oil from the flower is a delicate and painstaking task.

Late spring is the harvesting season and the 75-mile valley literally becomes a sea of roses. The rose gatherers, many of them schoolchildren, must begin work before sunrise, when the blossoms are moist with dew and the hot sun has not evaporated their oil. The gatherers pick the oily petals and place them in baskets tied to their waists. The petals are then quickly taken to the perfume distillery where they are boiled in water to make the oil rise to the surface. It takes more than 200 pounds of rose petals to produce just one ounce of attar, explaining why the substance and the perfume made from it are so expensive.

rice, cotton, grapes, watermelon, and tobacco. The grapes are used to make wine, some of the most prized wine in Eastern Europe. Bulgaria's vast vineyards make it the seventh-largest wine-producing nation on earth.

Bulgaria is the world's fourth-largest exporter of tobacco and Bulgarian cigarettes—with brand names like Shipka, Stewardess, and BT—are sold throughout Europe. Growing tobacco is hard work, as American writer Boyd Gibbons discovered when he joined Vangalia (van-GA-li-a), the wife of the family he was staying with, and other villagers in planting the crop one spring day in the Bulgarian village of Gorna Sushitsa:

Vangalia coils her braids on top of her head and wraps them with a white *kurpa* [KUR-pa] [a scarf]. We bend at the waist, a pile of plants in one hand, and with our thumbs stuff them in the mud a few inches

The annual Festival of Roses held at the start of the petal-picking season in June draws tourists from the world over. Women and children wear their folk costumes and wreaths of roses. A Rose Queen is selected and presides over dancing, singing, musical concerts, plays, and a parade of flowers. People wander through bright bazaars and arts and crafts exhibitions, eating jams made from rose petals and drinking rose petal brandy. In this valley roses are more than a livelihood—they are a way of life.

This pretty rose picker in Bulgaria's Valley of Roses pauses from her labor for a photographer. The rose petals must be picked in the early morning before their oil has been evaporated by the hot sun. The oil, known as attar, is used in perfumes and other products.
(UPI/Corbis-Bettmann)

apart. The mud is grainy, camouflaging sharp rocks, and my thumb is soon without cuticle, without feeling. Most of the villagers are out here on the hillsides punching in tobacco or hoeing, their conversation occasionally punctuated by the kibitzing of nightjars [nocturnal birds]. An Italian mower is cutting the hay, but most of the fields are too steep for anything but a *motika* [mo-TI-ka] [a heavy hoe] and muscle.

Walking home that evening, Vangalia smiles and says, "City girls are like eggs—they spoil in the sun. They have learned a lot, but they cannot endure this." Casually I touch my tender back, distinctly feeling the cracking of eggshells.

But just as much hard work goes into the cultivation of roses—which produce Bulgaria's most precious commodity, rose oil, known as attar, used to make some of the world's finest perfumes (see boxed feature).

Among livestock, the sheep is king. There are about nine million head of sheep, matching the country's human population. These animals are raised for their wool and meat. Pigs and chickens are also common, while bees are kept for their honey, which is used in making many a Bulgarian dish and dessert.

Timber from the mountains is a leading natural resource, but Bulgaria has little mineral wealth. Coal, copper, manganese ore, lignite, sulfur, and zinc are mined, but the deposits are small. Oil is also scarce, but in recent years a promising oil industry has been developing on the drilling sites of the Black Sea shelf in the cities of Varna (VAR-na) and Burgas (bur-GAS).

Another important source of power is Bulgaria's swift-running rivers. Hydroelectricity now accounts for a quarter of all electrical power. A nuclear power plant built at Kozloduy (koz-lo-DOOI) by the Soviets provides a fourth of all electricity for the country. Although these alternative source of power help, Bulgaria continues to be plagued by fuel and energy problems, as the last gas crisis dramatically illustrated.

Only a few years ago, Bulgaria had one of the fastest-expanding economics in Europe. By 1996, that economy was in shambles. Weak and fainthearted democratic leaders and stubborn and often corrupt Socialist leaders have both contributed to the problem. Before the economy can start to grow again, there is much to be done—a full commitment to privatization, the reduction of foreign debt, the return of stability to banking. If the government of President Petar Stoyano and the UDF can make progress on these fronts, Bulgaria may yet join its neighbors on the road to economic stability.

NOTES

P. 58   "First the bread, now the gas . . ." Associated Press News Service, May 27, 1996. CD NewsBank.

p. 58   "We buy only food . . . " Tracy Wilkinson, "Corruption and Poverty Feed Rebellion in Bulgaria," *Los Angeles Times,* January 23, 1997, p. A1.

p. 59   "We were supposed to be part . . . " *Washington Post,* July 7, 1996, p. A21. CD NewsBank.

p. 60   "We haven't had a Leszek Balcerowicz . . . " *Washington Post,* July 7, 1996, p. A21. CD NewsBank.

pp. 62–63 "Vangalia coils her braids . . . " Boyd Gibbons, "The Bulgarians," *National Geographic,* July 1980, p. 104.

8

Culture

*T*he Bulgarians have a right to be proud of their culture. As author Emil Georgiev (e-MIL ge-or-GI-ef) writes: "[they] were among the first [in Europe], after the decline of the ancient world, to found their own state and launch their own culture." Although Bulgaria's golden age of the arts ended early in its long history, culture remained a safe refuge from the invading hordes over the centuries, and kept the flame of the people's spirit alive through dark times. It is a culture that is uniquely democratic, meant to be enjoyed by all people, whether it be a poem praising the Bulgarian countryside, a church icon, or a folk song.

Language

The Bulgarian language was the first true Slavic tongue, and its history is deeply rooted in Slavic civilization. A pair of learned brother monks, Cyril

(SER-il) and Methodius (ma-THO-dee-us) created the Cyrillic (ser-IL-lik) alphabet to help found a Slavic church in Moravia, part of the present-day Czech Republic. The church did not survive, but the alphabet was brought to Bulgaria by the two monks' disciples and gave birth to the Bulgarian language. From there it spread throughout the Slavic lands.

Bulgarian is closely related to Russian, although its grammar is somewhat different from other Slavic languages, and in some ways resembles English. The language was banned under the Turks and became a tool for Bulgarian nationalism in the 19th century. It helped create a new contemporary literature that flourished after independence in 1878.

While Bulgarian is the official language of more than eight million Bulgarians, it is not the only language spoken in the country. Ethnic minorities also speak Turkish, Armenian, and Greek in different regions where these people have settled.

Literature

Bulgaria's golden age of literature flourished during the reign of Simeon I and the First Bulgarian Kingdom. Monks and other scholars turned out great religious and secular literature that spread Christianity and Slavic culture throughout Eastern Europe. When the first Bulgarian Kingdom collapsed early in the 11th century, the Byzantine Empire took over and foisted its own culture on Bulgaria. Bulgarian literature went "underground," returning to the villages and towns where it was kept alive in countless folktales, heroic sagas, proverbs (see boxed feature in chapter 9), riddles, and songs. This was primarily an oral tradition and the first Bulgarian book published in Cyrillic did not appear until 1651 in Rome.

Father Paisiy's *History of Slavo-Bulgarians* (1762) was the beginning of the national revival that reached its peak in the early 19th century. Writers and intellectuals not only wrote books but opened schools for Bulgarian children, published newspapers and textbooks, and collected folktales from the countryside—all in their native language.

Chitalishta (chi-TA-li-sta), a network of reading rooms open to all, first appeared in this period. More than mere reading rooms, they were intellectual and cultural centers where common people could meet, take classes in the arts, and even put on plays for the community. The chitalishta established the importance of the arts in a nation that was rediscovering itself and its culture. They remain an important part of literary and intellectual life in Bulgaria today.

The most read author of the nationalistic period was Ivan Vazov (1850–1921), often called the "father of modern Bulgarian literature." His most celebrated work is the novel *Under the Yoke* (1888), a fervid, patriotic novel about Bulgarian society on the brink of the April Uprising of 1876 against the Turks. It is one of the few Bulgarian novels that has been translated widely, including into English. Vazov is best known for this and other historical novels, but he also wrote stories, poems, and plays. His collected works fill over a hundred volumes.

As in many European countries, writers in Bulgaria in the early 20th century moved away from realism, a literary movement that pictures life as its actually is. Poets wrote a new kind of symbolist poetry filled with strange poetic images of death and decay. War and displacement haunted young writers like Dimcho Debelyanov (DIM-cho de-be-LYA-nof) (1887–1916) who expressed his love for his war-torn country in melancholy but beautiful verse. Debelyanov volunteered to fight in World War I and was killed in action.

Many Bulgarian writers were willing to fight, and if necessary, die for their country, but when the Communists took over, they discovered that an even sturdier heroism was needed. Life became a daily struggle to express themselves under what one writer calls "a Stalinist straitjacket." The writers who refused to become part of the Communist propaganda machine were arrested, tried, and either executed or sentenced to labor camps. Some chose suicide over living under such a repressive government. The poet Yosif Petrov (YO-sif pet-ROF) (1909–) was deprived of pen and paper in a labor camp and was forced to write poems in his head during these difficult years. He later recalled these prison poems and wrote them down for publication.

Another brave Bulgarian writer, Georgi Markov (ge-OR-gi MAR-kof) (1929–1978), fled his homeland and settled in England where he wrote such stinging critiques of the Communist regime as *Reports from Bulgaria from Abroad* and *The Truth That Killed*. Bulgarian Communist agents followed him on Waterloo Bridge in London one day and assassinated him by sticking the poisoned tip of an umbrella into his thigh.

The Bulgarian writers who stayed home and continued to write what was on their mind often eluded censorship by hiding their message in

A nation of great readers, Bulgaria is enjoying the new availability of books and magazines previously banned by the Communists. These browsers are checking out bookstalls in Sofia. (Rick Gerharter/Impact Visuals)

folklike fables and coded poetry. Among the most outspoken dissident writers in the 1960s was Blaga Dimitrova (BLA-ga di-mi-TRO-va) (1922–) whose poetry and prose attacked the corruption of the Communist system. In this excerpt from her novel *Journey to Oneself* (1965) she mocked the very language of the Communists:

> *Collective!* The endless speeches, reports, articles, interviews have planted that word in my mind—a parasite which I am powerless to uproot. What was "collective" about our life in that hut? We shared no common purpose, no common interests, no common rhythm. They tried to unify us through the medium of competitions: for the best kept room, the punchiest slogans, the brightest decorations. We were unimpressed.

While such writing did not get Dimitrova's work banned, a number of her books were not allowed to be published in Bulgaria. But her courage gained her an admiring public and in 1990, with the collapse of communism, she was elected a member of the National Assembly. In January 1992, at age 70, Blaga Dimitrova was elected vice president of Bulgaria, the first woman to ever hold so high an office in the government. She fought hard for issues affecting children and women as well as the rights of minorities such as the Turks. Frustrated by the political process, she resigned in 1994.

Today, Bulgarian literature continues to speak out against injustice, but ironically, the lack of government support for literature and the arts in the new Bulgaria has made it difficult for many writers to get their works published.

Music

Music and singing come as naturally to most Bulgarians as breathing. The country's rich heritage of folk music goes back to earliest times, but it continues to be an important part of Bulgarian life today. "It reflects, along with fragments of past history and extinct religion, the everyday life of thousands of villages. . . . good luck and bad, love, quarrels and death in such an intimate way, sometimes humorous, sometimes tender but always

Ljuba Welitsch (1913–1996)

B ulgaria has produced many great opera singers. Perhaps no Bulgarian singer made a more spectacular debut in the world of opera than did soprano Ljuba Welitsch.

Welitsch was born in Borissova (bo-RI-so-va), a town on the Black Sea coast. A singer and violinist from childhood, she first sang professionally in 1936 for the Graz Opera Company. After singing many roles in German opera houses, she made her debut at the Vienna Opera in the stirring role of Salome, the homicidal stepdaughter of King Herod in Richard Strauss's daring modern opera *Salome* in 1944. Strauss himself praised her performance, and the role became her favorite.

She was engaged by the Metropolitan Opera House in New York in 1949 to sing Salome and stunned the opening night audience with her acting and singing talent. One reviewer in the *New York Times* called her "an actress of individuality and power" as well as a great singer. The performance remains one of the most memorable in the history of that great opera house.

In the five years following *Salome,* Welitsch sang so much that she nearly ruined her voice. She could not sing starring roles. Although no longer a diva, she continued to sing and act in films, recordings, and on stage into the 1980s.

In 1956 she created a stir in the newspapers when at age 43 she married a 29-year-old traffic police officer who had helped her after an automobile accident. An extravagant woman who did nothing halfheartedly, Welitsch always lived up to her name, which in Bulgarian means "Love Great."

tense and vivid. . . ." writes author Elizabeth Marriage Mincoff in her book *Bulgarian Folksongs.*

The Bulgarian folk song has gained international acclaim through such touring groups as the Bulgaria A Cappella Choir and the all-women chorus Le Mystère des Voix Bulgares.

Almost as much loved as folk music is opera. The country boasts five opera houses and a number of great opera singers, especially bassos, who have gone on to international fame. Boris Christoff (bo-RIS HRIS-tof) (1914–1993) was best known for his unforgettable portrayal of the tortured czar Boris Gudonov in the Russian opera of the same name, and Ljuba Welitsch (LYOO-ba VE-lich) (see boxed biography) is remembered for her striking interpretation of the seductive and dangerous princess in *Salome.* Other Bulgarian-born opera singers who have achieved celebrity

Bulgarian-born opera singer Ljuba Welitsch in costume at the New York Metropolitian Opera House. She took the international opera world by storm in the 1940s with her stunning perform- ance as the seductive Salome, in the opera of the same name.
(Corbis-Bettmann)

beyond Eastern Europe are Nikolai Ghiaourov (ni-ko-LAI gya-OO-rof), Raina Kabaivanska (RAI-na ka-BA-i-van-ska), and Ghena Dimitrova (GE-na di-mi-TRO-va).

Bulgaria has twelve symphony orchestras, including the Sofia Philhar-monic and the Bulgarian National Radio Symphony, both of which perform during the annual Sofia Music Weeks from May 24 to July 2.

Bulgarian instrumental folk music is rich in rhythms and highly sophisticated meters and beats. The music is played on such unusual folk instruments as the *guida* (GAI-da), a kind of bagpipes; the *kaval* (ka-VAL), a wooden flute; and the *gadulka* (ga-DOOL-ka), a stringed instrument played with a bow that resembles a mandolin. The most popular Bulgarian folk dance is the *horo* (ho-RO), where dancers swirl around in a circle, holding hands.

Christo (1935–)

While other artists paint pictures or create sculptures, the Bulgarian-born artist known as Christo sees the whole world as material for his art. Since the early 1960s, this controversial artist has been leaving his eccentric mark on the landscapes of a dozen countries—a curtain dropped across a rugged valley in Colorado, giant umbrellas in Japan, the German Reichstag (a government building) wrapped in more than a million square feet of silver polypropylene fabric. His masterpiece may be a 24-mile fabric "fence" running along a stretch of California coastline.

He was born Christo Javashev (ya-VA-shef) in Gabrovo (GA-bro-vo), Bulgaria, where his father was a chemist and businessman. He attended Sofia's Fine Arts Academy and was studying in Prague, Czechoslovakia, in 1956 when the Hungarian Revolt broke out and was quickly crushed by the Soviets. Christo fled to the West to escape communism, and eventually settled in Paris where he made sculptures out of bottles and cans.

One of his first large-scale works was called *Iron Curtain—Wall of Oil Drums,* which were just that. He set it up on a Parisian street where it blocked traffic.

In 1964, Christo moved to New York City where his projects grew more and more grandiose. Some were too outlandish to actually complete, such as his plan to erect 48-foot high glass walls on every east-west highway in the United States. But others have been completed at enormous effort and cost, such as his covering of a one-million square-foot section of the Australian coastline with erosion control fabric and 36 miles of rope.

Some people think Christo's work is silly and a waste of money and resources, while others see it as brilliant commentary on the natural and human-made world. Christo himself sees both the obstacles and the

Art

Bulgarian art is less known to the outside world than is its music, but it has an equally impressive breath and range.

During the First Bulgarian Kingdom, artists and artisans expressed their faith in gorgeous church murals, frescoes, and small religious images painted on wood called icons. Many of these artworks can be seen today

triumphs as a part of each of his works. "For me esthetics is everything included in the process—the workers, the politics, the negotiations, the construction difficulty. . . . I'm interested in discovering the process. I put myself in dialogue with other people."

Like a general in battle, artist Christo gives orders to workers wrapping one of 11 islands in Biscayne Bay, Florida, in pink plastic. Christo's extravagant conceptual art works have been both praised and ridiculed by critics.
(UPI/Corbis-Bettmann)

in museums, churches, and monasteries. They bear the strong influence of Byzantine art, especially in their dark, vibrant colors.

Two of the most famous of 20th-century Bulgarian artists are conceptualist Christo (HRI-sto) (see boxed biography), who now lives in the United States, and painter Zlatya Boyadziev (ZLA-tia bo-ya-DJI-ef) (1903–1976), who lived and worked in Plovdiv. Boyadziev suffered a stroke in 1951, which affected his brain and the way he saw colors. His painting style changed dramatically and his later paintings are, in the words of one critic, "explosions of color, dazzling and highly evocative."

Today, many artists, along with writers, performers, singers, and musicians are finding it difficult to support themselves in post-Communist Bulgaria. While the Communists funded artists who painted in the realistic style they prized, artists who refused to compromise their vision could still get funding for state-commissioned murals and other public works of art. Today, ironically, that has all changed. "For the fine artists there is no structure of support," complains artist Ilia Petkov (i-LI-ya pet-KOF). "Private funds go after cheaper artists and look to support touristic artwork. I thought I was ready for the opportunities of democracy. Now I find I'm not prepared. . . ."

Theater

The theater is an integral part of Bulgarian life and culture. From the national theater in Sofia, established by the Communists, to the smallest village production, theater, like the other arts, belongs to the people. During the National Revival of the 19th century, theater was meant to rouse the people's feelings for patriotism and nationhood. In his novel *Under the Yoke*, Ivan Vazov describes with insight and humor the reactions of simple village folk to a local production of a stirring patriotic drama:

> Then came the third act. . . . Golos appears, dishevelled, ugly, tortured by remorse and wearing the fetters of the konak* [ko-NAK] prison. He is greeted by a hostile murmur from the audience. Angry looks pierce him. The Count reads him a letter in which the Countess includes him in her forgiveness, and breaks down again, tearing his hair, beating his breast. The audience sobs again unrestrainedly.
>
> Aunt Ghinka is also shedding tears, but wants to reassure the others. "There's nothing to cry about, Genevieve is alive in the forest!"
>
> Some of the old women, who don't know the play, speak up in surprise. "Heavens, Ghinka, is she really? Why don't somebody tell

---

*The governor's residence, seat of the local Turkish government.

him, poor man, and stop him crying?" said Granny Petkovistsa, while Granny Hadji Pavlyuvitse, unable to restrain herself, called out through her tears, "There, my boy, don't cry; your bride's alive!"

In the Communist era, playwrights and their audiences became more sophisticated. They used satire, disguised in the form of simple parables, to attack the repressive political system they lived under. The contemporary playwright Yordan Radichkov (yor-DAN ra-DICH-kof) (1929–) has had his plays performed in Western Europe and the United States. He also writes folklike tales and film scripts.

Film

The cinema got a late start in Bulgaria due to the interruptions of war and other calamities in the first decades of the 20th century. Vassil Gendov (va-SIL JEN-dof) directed the first Bulgarian film *Bulgarians Are Gallant* (1910) and the first talking film in 1933. For years he was the only Bulgarian film director and struggled under difficult circumstances to make his films.

The Communists nationalized and enlarged the Bulgarian film industry, but the films they produced were mostly dull historical epics meant to inspire the Bulgarians to make greater sacrifices for their Communist government. New and imaginative young directors appeared in the late 1950s making films that dealt with serious contemporary issues. Rangle Vulchanov's (RAN-gel vul-CHA-nof) *Sun and Shadow* (1962) and *The Peach Thief* (1964), directed by Vulo Radev (VU-lo RA-def), were the first Bulgarian films to be widely seen abroad. By the 1970s the Bulgarian film industry was turning out 20 features and 200 short films a year, including many animated films. Since the fall of communism, the industry has taken a nosedive. Without state funding, many directors have been unable to get money to make films, and some of Bulgaria's 271 movie theaters have been forced to close.

Bulgarian culture, one of the most pluralistic in Europe, has ironically been dealt a serious blow by democracy. Until Bulgaria is further along the road to a freer system of government and a stable economy, the arts will be just another casualty of the difficult transition from communism to democracy.

"Culture is burning in our part of the world," says artist Ilia Petkov. "But culture will rise from the ashes like the phoenix."

NOTES

p. 65   "[they] were among the first . . ." Naughton, p. 290.

p. 69   "*Collective!* The endless speeches . . ." Naughton, p. 319.

pp. 69–70   "It reflects, along with fragments . . ." Quoted in Assen Nicoloff, *Bulgarian Folklore* (Cleveland, Ohio: published by the author, 1983), p. 48.

p. 73   "For me esthetics is everything . . ." *Current Biography 1977* (New York: H. W. Wilson, 1978), p. 110.

p. 74   "For the fine artists there is no structure . . ." Eleanor Kennelly, "Pictures etched in his mind," *Washington Times*, January 4, 1996, C8. CD NewsBank.

pp. 74–75   "Then came the third act. . . ." Ivan Vazov, *Under the Yoke* (New York: Twayne, 1971), p. 91.

p. 76   "Culture is burning . . ." *Washington Times*, January 4, 1996, C8. CD NewsBank.

9

Daily Life

Since communism's fall, daily life in Bulgaria has become more and more of a struggle for survival. The majority of people live in poverty or near poverty. The middle class is virtually nonexistent. Professional people like doctors and lawyers face the same economic hardships as everyone else. The small privileged class that does exist did not get its wealth through education and hard work, but good connections within the small circle of former Communists. Is it any wonder most Bulgarians look toward the future with cynicism?

Education

Any hope for the future in Bulgaria may lie in its educational system. Education is a top priority in this small country, and school is part of daily life for every child from six to sixteen.

Under the Communists, children did not only learn in school but on the job, working part-time in factories and on farms at careers they were interested in pursuing. The government adapted schools to accommodate working parents, which included nearly every couple in the country. Students remained after school in study halls called *zanimalnia* (za-ni-MAL-nya) until parents could pick them up after work. There were even special boarding schools called *internat* (in-ter-NAT) for children whose parents, for whatever reasons, couldn't take care of them.

But if the literacy rate in Bulgaria today is among the world's highest, at nearly 100 percent, the Communists can take little credit for it. Education has been important to Bulgarians since the early 19th century. The father of modern Bulgarian education was Dr. Petar Beron (PE-tar be-RON), an emigrant from Romania. In 1824 he published the first school primer in the modern Bulgarian language. Before Beron, schools were modeled on the antiquated monastery system. He created a new, secular model for schools that made education more appealing and intelligible to youth. With the permission of the Turks, a school based on Beron's ideas opened in the city of Gabrovo in 1835. It was the first modern school to teach in Bulgarian.

Today, education begins early with four-fifths of all children aged three to six attending preschool. Elementary school goes to the eighth grade, during which time most students begin studying a foreign language, usually Russian, English, or German. High school, called gymnasium, often requires students to pass an entrance exam. Unlike those in the United States, Bulgarian high schools are highly specialized. Many of them focus on one area of learning—math, science, music, art, public health, or sports. There are also vocational schools that teach students a trade.

The top students from gymnasium go on to one of the 40 institutions of higher learning, which include 21 colleges and universities. The most distinguished of these is the University of Sofia, founded in 1888. There are also 268 technical colleges and schools for the arts.

In the post-Communist era, Bulgarians are reexamining the university system. Standards are being changed to allow more students to enter college and pursue a more flexible curriculum. Under communism, a university was free to those who qualified. More recently, the government has proposed tuition fees for all students. Many Bulgarians are opposed to these fees.

Bulgarian Proverbs

Wisdom in a Few Words

Proverbs are wise old sayings that most Americans relegate to the quaint past. Not so in Bulgaria. Proverbs are a proud part of Bulgarian folk literature that remains very much alive today. People quote proverbs to make a point, support an argument, or just to enliven the conversation. Authors and poets use familiar proverbs in their writing. Parents and teachers use them to teach a moral lesson to children.

Bulgarian proverbs are rich in humor, practical advice, and moral values. With more than 20,000 proverbs in the language, there is a proverb for every situation and occasion. These wise sayings not only help people, but reveal much about the Bulgarian character to the rest of the world.

Many proverbs, not surprisingly, use the language of agriculture. For example: "Every pear has a stem," which means "life is full of opportunity," or "Your mill grinds coarse," which means "You do not attend to your business." Other sayings show how highly the Bulgarians value education: "He who learns will succeed." Still others show a deep respect for age—"An old pot boils tasty broth"—or a certain fatalistic attitude towards life—."The world is a ladder; some climb up, others climb down."

One of the reasons Bulgarian proverbs are so rich in content is that many were borrowed from or influenced by other peoples including the Turks, the Greeks, the Romanians, the Persians, and the Armenians.

Here are some Bulgarian proverbs that might sound familiar to you and their English equivalents.

Bulgarian	English
Like cow, like calf.	Like father, like son.
Many midwives—a feeble infant.	Too many cooks spoil the broth.
Housework is never at an end.	A woman's work is never done.
Home today, dead tomorrow.	Here today, gone tomorrow.

Whatever disagreements there are over the future of education, few Bulgarians would argue about its importance. Perhaps the best proof of this is the fact that Bulgaria has set aside one day each year to honor its educators. The Day of Letters (May 24) is a holiday that celebrates learning and knowledge. Students bring flowers to their teachers. Authors and illustrators of children's books read from their works, talk to students, and autograph books. There are exhibits of books and arts and crafts and performances of plays and concerts.

Holidays and Celebrations

The Day of Letters is just one of the many celebrations that fill the Bulgarian calendar. In the post-Communist era, the two major Christian holidays, Christmas and Easter, have taken on a greater significance. The orthodox Christmas is celebrated over three days from December 24 through 26. Caroling and good eating mark the season. The Bulgarian Santa Claus, Father Frost, doesn't make his appearance until New Year's Day when he and his helper, Snow White, place gifts under Christmas trees. New Year's Day is the time of another curious custom. Children are allowed to "beat" their elders on the back with decorated dogwood branches. The flowering dogwood symbolizes good health and happiness in the new year. Later, during the New Year's feast, the father or the oldest person in the family lights the yule log, a traditional, large log burned during the Christmas season. The lighting of the log is an assurance of long life. Easter is a more solemn occasion. After church services, families visit the graves of their loved ones and leave flowers.

Other celebrations predate the Christian era and are mostly associated with Bulgaria's rich agricultural past. None is older than *Trifon Zarezan* (TRI-fon za-re-ZAN) or Vinegrower's Day (January 14), which dates all the way back to Thracian times. Farmers prune their grape vines on this day and spill wine over the shoots to ensure a good growing season. Men of the village march through the streets wearing large grotesque masks and cowbells to frighten away evil spirits. A feast is then held in a meadow with much music, drinking, and dancing, all presided over by a local man who has been chosen to be "Vine King."

Shepherds and herdsmen have their holiday, too. On Saint George's Day, local people and tourists alike flock to the mountains where lambs are roasted whole over a spit. Traditionally after the lamb is eaten, some of its bones are buried in an anthill to symbolize that the sheep will

Masks and outlandish costumes are a central part of several age-old Bulgarian holidays. This terrifying creature is actually a youth dressed to represent a wild animal. At the end of this New Year's procession he will be given gifts of money and goods from his fellow townspeople. (Corbis-Bettmann)

multiply like ants. Other bones are hurled into the nearest river to signify that lamb's milk will flow like water.

Other holidays commemorate the more recent past. National Day of Freedom and Independence (March 3) honors all—both Bulgarians and foreigners—who fought to liberate the country from the Ottoman Turks in the Russo-Turkish War of 1877–78. On Martyr's Day (June 6) Bulgarians remember all who have died in the cause of Bulgarian patriotism. Chief among these is the great national poet Hristo Botev (HRI-sto BO-tef) (1848-1876) who died fighting the Turks during the 1876 uprising on June 6.

Sports and Leisure

The Bulgarians are a hardy people, and athletics are an integral part of their lives. Competitive sports began with the Thracians, whose love of wrestling and gymnastics is part of a tradition that continues in Bulgaria today. The strive for athletic excellence can be clearly seen in the country's Olympic record. Bulgaria was one of only 13 nations to take part in the first modern Olympic Games held in Athens, Greece, in 1896. Bulgarian athletes have won numerous medals in track and field, weight lifting, wrestling, and most recently, rhythmic gymnastics. At the 1996 Olympics in Atlanta, Georgia, the world champion Bulgarian women's rhythmic gymnastics team won the silver medal with a spectacular routine using balls and ribbons, put in motion to the sounds of Bulgarian folk music.

The country's most popular spectator sport, as in many European countries, is soccer. When the Bulgarian soccer team defeated Germany in the quarter finals of the World Cup in 1994 it was a cause for national celebration. Top soccer players are as popular as rock stars in the United States, none more so than former player Petar Stoyano, who is now Bulgaria's president. Other popular sports are basketball, especially for women, volleyball, and tennis.

When Bulgarians go on vacation they generally head for one of two locations—the mountains or the seacoast. In the Rhodope and Rila Mountains visitors hike and camp in the summer and ski and toboggan in the winter. At the sandy beaches along the Black Sea coast vacationers love to swim, fish, or row a boat.

For those too sick or tired to do anything so strenuous there are numerous spas or health resorts surrounding more than 200 mineral springs. Their restorative waters are said to alleviate everything from arthritis to skin disease.

Food and Drink

The Bulgarian national cuisine has been heavily influenced by its neighbors, the Greeks and former masters the Turks. Dishes adapted from the Greeks include *sarmi* (sar-MI), stuffed grape leaves; *banitsa* (BA-ni-tsa), a crusty pastry containing spinach and cheese; and *mousaka* (mu-sa-KA), a hash made of lamb and potatoes. Even the most anti-Turkish Bulgarian probably enjoys a morning cup of Turkish coffee, a strong and very sweet beverage. It takes a stronger stomach to drink the alcoholic *boza* (bo-ZA), a thick gray ale made out of fermented grains.

But there is one popular food that is uniquely Bulgarian—yogurt. This dairy product made out of cow's or sheep's milk combined with bacteria, was first made here centuries ago. While most Americans eat yogurt as a lunch or snack, Bulgarians eat it at nearly every meal—as a food, a soup, a side dish, or a sauce. They do so for good reasons. Yogurt has been shown to be one of the healthiest of all foods and is even said to prolong the lives of people who make it a regular part of their diet. There may be something to this, for Bulgaria, a nation of yogurt-eaters, has the greatest population of people over the age of 100 in all Europe.

NOTES

p. 79   "Every pear has a stem," Nicoloff, p. 243.
p. 79   "Your mills grind coarse," Nicoloff, p. 242.
p. 79   "He who learns will succeed," Nicoloff, p. 269.
p. 79   "An old pot boils tasty broth," Nicoloff, p. 256.
p. 79   "The world is a ladder . . ." Nicoloff, p. 263.
p. 79   "Like cow, like calf," Nicoloff, p. 246.
p. 79   "Many midwives—a feeble infant," Nicoloff, p. 254.
p. 79   "Housework is never at an end," Nicoloff, p. 251.
p. 79   "Home today, dead tomorrow," Nicoloff, p. 260.

10

The Cities

*N*ot so many years ago cities were a small part of Bulgarian life. The vast majority of people were farmers living in villages and towns. Today, that situation has changed drastically. Thanks to the industrialization of the country under the Communists, two-thirds of all Bulgarians now live in urban areas. In 1946, the year a Communist government was installed, there were only two cities in the country that had a population over 100,000—the capital Sofia and Plovdiv. In 1990, the year communism ended, there were 10 cities that had populations higher than 250,000.

Though they may have been relatively small for centuries, Bulgaria's cities are survivors. Wars, invasions, fires, and other catastrophes have razed them many times, but they have always risen again, often with new names and new masters. The cities of Bulgaria are a symbol of the resilient spirit of their people.

Sofia is studded with old churches, museums, and monuments. One of the most famous is Alexander Nevski Cathedral, named after the great Russian hero who freed his people from the Teutonic Knights in the 13th century. (Balkan Tours)

Sofia: "Ever Growing, Never Old!"

Sofia (population 1.38 million, 1995 estimate)[*] is Bulgaria's largest city, lying in the foothills of the Vitosha (VI-to-sha) Mountains in the far western region of the country, 1,820 feet (555 m) above sea level. As its motto proudly states, Sofia is an intriguing mix of the old and the new. And "old" means old. Founded nearly 2,000 years ago by the Roman emperor Trajan, it is the second oldest capital city in Europe after Athens, Greece.

Sofia's location as a trade route to Istanbul and its temperate climate impressed Emperor Constantine, and he almost made it the capital of his eastern empire around A.D. 300. If he had, the city may have been better fortified and escaped the wrath of Attila the Hun and his hoard who invaded and destroyed it about A.D. 450.

The city was rebuilt by Emperor Justinian I who made it part of the Byzantine Empire and named it Triaditsa (tri-A-di-tsa). The Bulgars conquered the city in 809 and renamed it Sredets (sre-DETS). It soon became the center of Slavic and Balkan culture.

The Byzantines retook the city in 1018 and eventually gave it the name Sofia, in honor of Saint Sofia, whose cathedral was built centuries earlier in the heart of the city by the Romans. Sophia, as the name is spelled in Greek, was the daughter of the emperor Justinian. According to legend, Sophia was incurably ill and her father brought her to the hot springs at the foot of Mount Vitosha, where shepherds cured their sick sheep by submerging them in the restorative waters. Sophia was cured in the same manner, and Justinian built a fortress on the spot to commemorate the miraculous event. It still stands today in the center of modern Sofia.

But no miracle could save the city from the invading Turks who occupied it in 1382. The Ottomans built their onion-domed mosques alongside Christian churches, changing the skyline of the ancient city forever. Sofia became the residence of Bulgaria's Turkish governors and only became part of a free Bulgaria again in 1878, the year of national independence, when it was also named the new capital.

From a small town of 20,000 souls, Sofia has grown into a metropolis of more than a million people in just a century. Today one in every nine Bulgarians lives in Sofia, and 20 percent of Bulgarian industry is located here.

---

[*] All populations, unless noted, are 1990 estimates.

People throughout Bulgaria are feeling the economic squeeze of recent years. Elderly residents on a tight budget make a careful selection from produce in a Sofia street market. (Sean Sprague/Impact Visuals)

Despite the changes that have made it into a modern and very crowded city, there are many impressive reminders of Sofia's glorious past. The Saint Alexander Nevski Cathedral with its crypt full of priceless icons is in the oldest part of the city. Nearby is Saint Sophia and another ancient church, Saint George, whose red brick rotunda was built in the fourth century.

Sofia is a city of museums and monuments. Besides the great National Museum, there are the Museum of Ecclesiastical History, the Museum of the Revolutionary Movement, the Archaeological Museum, and the National Library. Among its most striking monuments are the Monument to the Red Army and the mausoleum of Georgi Dimitrov, Bulgaria's first Communist leader. The seat of Bulgarian government and education, Sofia is home to the National Assembly building, the University of Sofia, and the Bulgarian Academy of Sciences.

When a visitor wants to sit back and relax amid nature in this city, he or she has some 400 parks to choose from. Several boulevards are paved with glazed yellow bricks that might make visitors think they are on the road to the Emerald City of Oz. But grim reality exists side by side with fantasy. On the outskirts of the city are dozens of high-rise apartment buildings that are home to the many workers who have come from the countryside in recent decades to work in Sofia's numerous factories and plants that produce textiles, chemicals, glasses, and electronic goods.

Bulgaria's Second City: Plovdiv

Only 90 miles southeast of Sofia on the Maritsa River lies Plovdiv (population 379,000), Bulgaria second-largest city. But Plovdiv is second to none in ancient history. An archaeologist's dream, the city has many Roman ruins. The most impressive of these is an amphitheater that once seated 3,000 spectators until Attila the Hun rode through and destroyed a portion of it. Enough of the theater remains, however, to hold concerts and other cultural events each summer. There is also a Roman forum, a restored sacrificial pyre where offerings were burned to appease the gods, two watchtowers and a sixth-century gate, and a good portion of the ancient city walls.

Buildings of more recent times have been put to good use, too. A national revival building from 1847 houses the Ethnographic[*] Museum, while a Greek Revival building is home to the Archaeological Museum, which contains a stunning collection of Thracian art objects. Another fascinating museum is the Museum of the National Revival Period that traces the inspirational story of Bulgaria's final struggle against the Turks.

But Plovdiv also has a more contemporary face, typified by the International Fair held here every September. Because of its central location, Plovdiv is even more of a transportation hub than Sofia. Textile, food processing, and petrochemical plants dominate its economy while its medical institute and agricultural school make it an educational center, too.

Varna and Burgas: Cities by the Sea

Bulgaria's 175-mile Black Sea coast is a center for tourism, off-shore oil drilling, shipping, and fishing. The country's two major ports, Varna and Burgas, are located here.

---

[*] The science of ethnology deals with different racial or cultural groups of people and their distinguishing characteristics.

This beautiful 19th-century National Revival building houses the Ethnographic Museum in Plovdiv, Bulgaria's second-largest city. (Balkan Tours)

The Ancient Gold of Varna

One fall day in 1972 a tractor driver was digging a trench for an electric cable near the city of Varna when he came upon a treasure trove of old bracelets, tools, and squares of shiny yellow sheet metal. When he brought them to Varna's National Museum, archaeologists were amazed to discover that the sheet metal was gold dating back to prehistoric times.

What puzzled museum workers was that no gold objects had ever been found before from this period, known generally as the Copper Age. They were, in fact, the oldest gold objects, to that time, ever found on earth, dating back to possibly 4600 B.C. A full-scale excavation was soon organized and over the next eight years a total of about 2,000 gold objects were found, including gold necklaces, breastplates, bracelets, and even the gold-encased handle of a stone ax. Most of the objects were part of an ancient cemetery, buried along with the dead to use in the afterlife. Some of the graves contained no bodies but were cenotaphs—monuments in memory of a dead person who is buried elsewhere. These graves contained clay face masks adorned with golden jewelry.

Experts believe the early people who mastered this art of gold making, passed the knowledge on to the Thracians who succeeded them in Bulgaria. "[They] discovered for perhaps the first time in human history," writes archaeologist Colin Renfrew, "the attractive properties—the dazzle, the freedom from corruption, the allure—of that noblest of metals: gold."

Varna (population 315,000) lies in the north and is Bulgaria's third-largest city and one of its oldest. The oldest known trove of golden objects was discovered here in 1972 (see boxed feature). Varna was founded by the Greeks in 580 B.C. and named Odessus. In A.D. 679 the Bulgars defeated the Byzantines at Varna in a decisive battle. The Turks seized the city in 1391 and made it a thriving seaport. The last major battle to uproot the Turks from Europe was fought here in 1444 and lost by Polish king Ladislaus III. Varna's location made it an important naval base for the British and French during the Crimean War (1853–56).

While shipping and summer resorts are important to the city's economy, there is also a major cotton textile industry in Varna. Foodstuffs, soap, ceramics, and machinery are also produced.

Burgas (population 205,000) lies further south on the coast. It is Bulgaria's most important fishing port and home of the ocean-going fishing fleet. Burgas is a very young city for this ancient land, founded in the 18th century on the site of a 14th-century town. South of the city is a center of petrochemical works, the largest in Bulgaria.

Veliko Turnovo and Gabrovo: Beauty and Laughter

In north central Bulgaria lie two of the country's most interesting towns. Veliko Turnovo on the Yantra (YAN-tra) River was Bulgaria's medieval capital and still retains the grace and dignity of a royal city. Here are the ancient fortress on Tsarevets (TSA-re-vets) Hill with its sturdy battle towers and the Holy Trinity Monastery founded in 1070. But what attracts visitors to Veliko Turnovo as much as its history is the natural beauty of the town's surroundings and how they blend in with the buildings. One writer has called it "an entire island of beauty, with whitewashed houses and red-tiled roofs overlooking splendid national revival buildings."

Gabrovo (population 81,000), 30 miles to the south, is also a capital but of a very different kind. It prides itself as the "world capital of Humor." Known for their way with a joke and a funny story, the people of Gabrovo began the world's first Festival of Humor and Satire in 1965. Nine years later the Home of Humor and Satire opened its doors. Statues of Charlie Chaplin and the humorous but heartbreaking knight Don Quixote stand outside. Inside are rooms full of whimsical artworks from many countries.

There is a more serious side to Gabrovo. It was here that Bulgarian industry began in the early years of the 20th century. Today the city is a major center for textiles, including everything from silk and cotton to buttons and thread.

More Cities Worth Knowing

Each of Bulgaria's cities has its own story to tell. There is Stara Zagora (STA-ra za-GO-ra, population 165,000) founded by the Thracians, that was completely destroyed during the Russo-Turkish War and remade as a thoroughly modern city. The cigarettes made in Stara Zagora are smoked throughout Europe.

Pleven (PLI-ven, population 138,000) in north central Bulgaria was the site of a decisive victory for the Russians in the Russo-Turkish War. Its fall after four months of fighting led the Turks to call for an armistice that ended the war.

Another strategic site during the war was Shumen (SHOO-men, population 111,000) in northeastern Bulgaria, formerly named Kolarovgrad in honor of Communist leader Kolarov (ko-LA-rof) who was born there. It is also the site of Bulgaria's largest mosque, built in 1649.

The cities of Bulgaria have, like their people, endured many hardships, but they continue to thrive. As more and more Western visitors enter this little-known land for the first time, it is the cities, with their rich past, that are likely to first win their hearts.

NOTES

p. 90   "[They] discovered for perhaps the first time . . ." Colin Renfrew, "Ancient Bulgaria's Golden Treasures," *National Geographic*, July 1980, p. 129.

p. 91   "an entire island of beauty . . ." *New York Times*, Travel Section, June 23, 1996, p. 18.

Present Problems and Future Solutions

"We are born with tears and with tears we die," says an old Bulgarian proverb. The people of this small, beleaguered country are used to suffering. They have borne with much in their long, tearful history, but they have also achieved much. There is a strong practical streak in the Bulgarians that may well help them to persevere and deal with the many problems that plague them in the 1990s and beyond. The new coalition government is earnestly seeking to find solutions to the problems of the past and present to forge a better future. Here are some of those problems and their possible solutions.

The Economy

No bigger problem faces the new Bulgarian government than the economy. Its downward spiral over the past several years has affected every aspect of

Bulgarian life and society. The miserable conditions it created led to the demonstrations and dissent that eventually brought down the socialist government. It could bring down the latest government unless its leaders take action to improve things—and quickly.

"We wish to restore the confidence of the Bulgarian people in our state institutions, the Bulgarian lev [currency, pronounced LEF], Bulgarian banks, Bulgarian goods, as well as the confidence of foreign investors, international lending institutions, and foreign governments in our country," says Ivan Kostov, head of the UDF, the big winner in the April 1997 elections.

So far, the government seems to have its priorities right. Even before the election, the caretaker government set up by President Stoyanov moved to alleviate, if not completely eliminate, food and fuel shortages, while stabilizing the currency, which had been weakened by spiraling inflation.

To regain the confidence and support of the International Monetary Fund,[*] a fixed exchange-rate system has been established that will hopefully bring inflation under control and restore confidence in the lev. A currency board has also been established.

While the immediate fruits of these economic changes may be more misery, economists predict that the economy should start to stabilize. If the Bulgarian people believe and trust their leaders, they should be able to stick the course this time and move toward a better economic future with more jobs, a stable currency, and an improved standard of living.

There is no getting around the fact that Bulgaria is one of the last countries to emerge from the bonds of Communist thinking and has a difficult transition ahead. However, it can look to the support and encouragement of the West and other countries in the region who are willing to help if Bulgaria will only help itself.

Apathy and Emigration

Bulgaria, according to leading journalist Petko Bocharovo (PET-ko bu-CHA-ro-vo), suffers from "an absence of a feeling of national belonging. This, here is a population. This is not a nation."

Certainly communism and the bureaucracy that grew up around it, made people apathetic politically for decades. What is contributing further

---

[*] The International Monetary Fund is an organization of more than 145 nations that helps its members experience economic growth. Its headquarters are in Washington, D.C.

to this lack of national feeling is an alarmingly low birthrate. While other ethnic groups are growing, the Bulgarian population has been decreasing. There are several reasons for this. Peasant farms have been traditionally small and unable to support more than one or two children. The high percentage of working women has also made parenthood and child bearing less desirable to many couples. The Communist government tried to encourage more children by offering family allowances and generous maternity leaves for expectant mothers since the 1960s, but there was little change in the birthrate.

It is more than a low birth rate, however, that caused the population of Bulgaria to drop from nearly 9 million to 8.5 million in just one year. The youth of the country, seeing no opportunity for jobs and a productive future, have been leaving their homeland in record numbers in the 1990s.

Over 450,000 people, including skilled professionals, have left since 1992 and only about an eighth of this number is expected to return. Most émigrés have settled in France, Germany, Austria, the United States, and Canada.

Without the best and brightest of a generation, Bulgaria's future is in question. President Stoyanov and the new government realize this and are trying to keep more young people from leaving home by promising them a better future. But it will take more than rhetoric to keep them in Bulgaria or bring back those who have tasted the fruits of democracy and free enterprise abroad. As one 18-year-old student put it after the Socialists stepped down, "I don't have very much faith in the future. Regardless of which government we have, I will try very hard to get out of Bulgaria."

Human Rights

Compared to its neighbors in the former Yugoslavian republics, Bulgaria's internal ethnic problems seem minor. But they do exist. While ethnic Turks have fared far better in post-Communist Bulgaria than in the days of Todor Zhivkov's "Bulgarization" campaign, economics has proved to be as difficult an obstacle to surmount as politics once was for the Turkish population. Unemployment and low living standards led to a minor exodus of 40,000 Turks in 1992. The rise of the Movement for Rights and Freedom, a Turkish political party, has improved relations and gained new rights for Turks, but tensions still exist between the two groups. A small

Despair and uncertainty are etched on the faces of this ethnic Turkish grandfather and his grandchild. They wait with their belongings to cross the border into Turkey in 1989. Economic depression and government policy forced hundreds of thousands of Bulgarian Turks to leave in the 1980s. Despite improved conditions and greater tolerance today, many Turks still feel they are second-class citizens.
(Reuters/Corbis-Bettmann)

but vocal group of nationalist extremists cries out regularly for an end to Turkish schools where Turkish is spoken and even wants Turkish names to be withheld from Turks who were "Bulgarized" in the 1980s.

Slightly less visible but also targets of prejudice are the Gypsies. These nomadic people make up 3.4 percent of the population and are Bulgaria's second largest minority group.

Many Bulgarians see Gypsies as parasites, criminals, and undesirables. In Bulgaria they have mainly given up the colorful, wandering life of the past and live mostly in urban slums where the men are largely unemployed and few of the children go to school. The first national political organization of Gypsies called Roma, for Romanies, was set up in the fall of 1992. Like the Turks, some Gypsies are realizing that until they organize themselves politically their needs will not be met by a government preoccupied with its own problems.

National Security

Considering Bulgaria's close relationship with the Soviet Union under communism, it is not surprising that it was not among the first Eastern Eurpean nations clamoring to gain entrance into NATO. So it came to many in the West as a shock when in February 1997 the Bulgarian National Assembly reversed the position it has held since 1989 and unanimously voted to request admission into NATO.

Bulgaria's reasons for wanting to join the organization of Western nations may be less for protection from Russian aggression than to align itself more firmly with the Western countries it would like to emulate politically and economically. "With its decision, the government responded to the desire of the prevailing majority of the Bulgarian citizens who feel as an inseparable part of the free world," said President Stoyanov in a statement. "These are the countries which we would like to resemble in terms of democracy, economy, living standards. These are the countries our children are looking at."

In July 1997 the Czech Republic, Poland, and Hungary were officially invited to join NATO as full members. With Russia agreeing to form a joint NATO-Russia security council, the possibility of Bulgaria becoming a future member of the organization is a real one.

The symbolism of these children playing on the monument of the Unknown Soldier in downtown Sofia is inescapable. Will the future hold peace and prosperity for Bulgaria or more of the violence and strife that has plagued this small country for centuries? (Reuters/Corbis-Bettmann)

If Bulgaria does in time become a member of NATO, it will undoubtedly find a new bond with its neighbors Greece and Turkey, who are already NATO members. While its relations with Greece have been friendly as far back as 1980, things have not gone so smoothly with Turkey, for whom Bulgaria's treatment of ethnic Turks has been a dividing issue for years.

But the neighbors Bulgaria has had the most problems with are the former Yugoslav republics. There are still those Bulgarians who want to annex Yugoslav Macedonia, a territory that Bulgaria once owned. The internal strife in the republics of Serbia and Bosnia may have made the annexation more tempting for the Bulgarian government, although it denies any such intentions.

Whatever threats to national security Bulgaria might feel, especially from Russia, are further intensified by the lack of a strong national defense. The Bulgarian People's Army (BPA) has been severely reduced by a floundering economy that cannot support an expensive defense system. Whether a powerful military presence is necessary in post-Communist Europe is a question for debate within Bulgaria today.

Crime

The internal threat of violent crime is more a concern for most Bulgarians than the threat of a foreign invasion. As throughout Eastern Europe, crime, especially organized crime, has been steadily on the rise since the fall of communism. In 1990 the rate of all major crimes—including homicide, burglary, and rape—were way above the rates in the 1980s when Communist repression kept a firm sense of order.

Corporate crime and political corruption have given free enterprise a bad name for some Bulgarians, although many of those who have benefited have been former Communists. Politicians and businessmen alike have brazenly stolen from the businesses they have owned. Former president Zhelev's warning in 1995 of "a mafia state" in Bulgaria several years ago seems all the more real today. "In our country, the mafia works under the cover of security and insurance companies," claims parliament member Yordan Sokolov. "It is racketeering on a really large scale. The criminal groups control whole branches of industry."

Honest and respectable business people, from store owners to old ladies selling newspapers on the street corners, are forced to pay "protection insurance" or suffer a beating from the payoff men—thick-necked "wrestlers" in black leather jackets.

The boldness of the criminal element in Bulgaria today was strikingly dramatized in October 1996 by the assassination of former prime minister Andrei Lukanov, who was gunned down in broad daylight outside his home. In another headline crime, a small Sofia airline was besieged by crooks who seized the office and people inside as hostages and demanded $2 million. Fortunately, the plan failed and they were later caught and arrested.

Clamping down on crime is a high priority for the new coalition government but with more than 10 organized crime groups in Sofia alone, the government has its work cut out for it. Some measures already taken have made a difference, including tighter gun control laws,* better custom checkpoints to cut down on the smuggling of drugs and other contraband, and close cooperation with the International Crime Police Organization (Interpol). There is even a new radio call-in show called *No to the Fear* where people can talk to the host about the problems of crime they face daily.

Perhaps what will help most in the war against crime is the example of Bulgarian government and business leaders who exhibit personal integrity and do not consider themselves and their friends "above the law."

Health

Bulgaria was once a shining example of state-managed health care in the Communist world. With the breakdown of that system and the devastating economy of the past few years, all this has changed drastically. The health budget virtually disappeared and by the end of 1996 the situation had reached crisis level. Regional hospitals had closed. Those that stayed open were informed that no medical supplies would be coming soon, because the government didn't have the money to pay for them.

---

*Parliament members and government officials were until recently allowed by law to carry guns.

"It's a very, very bad situation," said one neurosurgeon at Queen Jovanna (yo-A-na), Sofia's most prestigious hospital. "For two weeks we have had to tell patients they have to pay for their own cotton, syringes, needles—everything that is needed for emergency treatment except the doctors' salaries."

Those salaries were scandalously low, even by Eastern European standards. The best Bulgarian surgeons earned about $60 a month. Things had gotten so bad at the Queen Jovanna that doctors were ordered to send home all but the sickest patients and perform no operations.

This is not what the government had in mind when it created a National Health Council in 1991. Their goal was to replace the authoritarian Communist health-care system with one where the patient had some choice in choosing a doctor or a hospital. Yet with a shrinking budget and no state funds, donations and patients' fees have not been enough to achieve this goal.

Despite some of the healthiest old people in all Europe, Bulgaria is not a healthy country. Over a third of all women and a fourth of all men are overweight. They overeat on a diet rich in fats and sugar, smoke too much, and too frequently abuse alcohol. Strokes kill a higher percentage of people in Bulgaria than anywhere else in the world. Many of these deaths are preventable if people would change their lifestyle.

Old habits die hard, especially in such a tradition-bound society as Bulgaria, but health education, both in school and among the general public would help immensely. Unfortunately, with so many other problems facing the medical community, it may be some time before preventative medicine becomes a priority.

The Environment

Another major health hazard in Bulgaria comes from the air, the water, and the very soil. According to a 1990 study, more than a third of the population is at risk from environmental pollution. The Communists left a terrible legacy on this land of once untouched natural beauty. They poisoned the land with uncontrolled use of pesticides. They polluted rivers with industrial waste and sewage. They cut down two-thirds of Bulgaria's primary forest with unregulated lumbering.

Two Bulgarians in America

E lena Atanassova (e-LE-na a-ta-NA-sova) is a student at Eastern Tennessee State University majoring in marketing. Middle-aged Kiril (known as Kiki) Todorov (KI-ril to-do-ROF) commutes from his Connecticut home to his job as a bartender in a New York City restaurant. Their lives are very different, but Elena and Kiki have two important things in common. They are both Bulgarians living in the United States and neither has any interest in returning home.

Kiki was a professional soccer player and an optician* when he first decided to escape from Communist Bulgaria to a freer life in the West back in 1967. He failed twice, but finally escaped through Yugoslavia with a fake passport. He lived and worked in Austria for two years before emigrating to Canada, where his brother, who had also fled Bulgaria, was living. He eventually moved to the United States.

Elena Atanassova, 22, sees a new life for herself in the United States. She is a student at Eastern Tennessee State University and hopes to go to medical school in the future.
(Elena Atanassova)

---

* a person who makes eyeglasses and other optical instruments

Kiki's brother is planning to return to Bulgaria, possibly to stay. Kiki has no interest in joining him. "I feel sorry for them [the Bulgarians at home]," he says. "There are many good people there, educated people. But it's going to take a long time for things to improve."

Elena, who has only been here two years, agrees. "Things will get better, eventually," she believes. "But it will take too much time. I don't want to waste my life there."

Instead she would like to continue her schooling in the United States and one day fulfill her dream of going to medical school. If that doesn't work out, she would like to work in marketing in a health-related field. Her father, who has been in the United States for six months, plans to go back to Bulgaria. Her mother and stepfather have no plans to leave their homeland. Elena stays in touch with relatives back home through E-mail.

Although it is easy to criticize the government, Elena sees the nation itself as the bigger problem. "People don't want to work that much," she says. "They had 45 years of being lazy under communism and don't want to change."

Will Kiki return to Bulgaria? "Yes, someday to show my wife my country," he says. "But not to stay."

Kiril (Kiki) Todorov, 57, escaped from Communist Bulgaria over 30 years ago. Although the Communists are no longer in power, he has no intention of going back to his homeland and giving up the good life he has made for himself in the United States. (Kiril Todorov)

While factory pollution and motor-vehicle emissions pollute the air in Sofia and other cities, metallurgical works and mining contaminate wider regions with poisonous lead, mercury, and sulfur dioxide. Children are particularly vulnerable to the pollution and many suffer from environmentally induced respiratory diseases and damaged immune systems that make them prey to a host of illnesses.

Not all of Bulgaria's pollution is home grown. The worst polluted city in the nation in the 1980s was the port of Ruse where water and air had been saturated by a chlorine and sodium plant directly across the Danube River in the town of Giurgiu (GLOOR-giyu), Romania. Communist officials refused to address the issue and make the Romanians accountable because they wanted to preserve good relations with their neighbor to the north. Such political diplomacy cost the people of Ruse dearly. Environmentalists found the Giurgiu plant directly responsible for an increase in the number of premature babies, miscarriages, and deformed children in the Bulgarian city. In desperation, over 3,000 families left Ruse to protect their children and themselves. But with as many as two-thirds of Bulgarians suffering some health problems from pollution, one wonders just where it is safe to live.

However, the picture is not entirely bleak. In 1991, Bulgaria joined Romania, Turkey, and Russia in a joint study of rising pollution in the Black Sea. Individual Bulgarians have stood up against the tide of pollution in significant ways. Thirty-one-year-old Albena Simeonova (al-BE-na si-me-O-no-va) has campaigned successfully against the building of nuclear power plants in his country. For his efforts he was honored with the Green Prize for Europe in 1996, awarded by a U.S. foundation.

As Bulgaria enters a new phase of leadership, it is hoped that the government will take the steps to repair the environment that until now have been more diligently pursued by individuals and small groups.

Like a hero in one of its fanciful folktales, Bulgaria has suffered many ordeals and setbacks in its quest for happiness. Slaying the dragon of communism has proved far more difficult than at first thought. A magical conjurer, this dragon has been able to transform itself time and again to escape destruction. The beautiful princess in the castle tower, like a mirage, seems all but unattainable. But if this fabled land of ancient glory and present woe can put aside despair, fear, and apathy, and believe in itself, it can yet grasp its destiny like a shining sword and struggle onward to a well-deserved happy ending.

NOTES

p. 93   "We are born with tears and with tears we die." Nicoloff, p. 272.

p. 94   "We wish to restore the confidence . . ." *New York Times*, May 8, 1997, p. A12.

p. 94   "an absence of a feeling . . ." Smale, Associated Press News Service, July 21, 1996. CD NewsBank.

p. 95   "I don't have very much faith . . ." Wilkinson, *Los Angeles Times*, January 23, 1997. CD NewsBank.

p. 97   "With its decision, the government . . ." "Bulgaria wants to join NATO." Associated Press News Service, February 17, 1997. CD NewsBank.

p. 99   "In our country, the mafia works . . ." Gregory Katz, "International Crime," *Dallas Morning News*, December 17, 1995, p. A1. CD NewsBank.

p. 101   "It's a very, very bad situation . . ." *New York Times*, December 25, 1996, p. A13.

p. 103   "I feel sorry for them . . ." Kiril Todorov in an interview with the author, August 30, 1997.

p. 103   "Things will get better . . ." Elena Atanassova in an interview with the author, July 15, 1997.

p. 103   "People don't want to work . . ." Atanassova interview.

p. 103   "Yes, someday to show my wife . . ." Todorov interview.

Chronology

c. 4000 B.C.	The Thracians arrive in present-day Bulgaria and establish their civilization.
c. 300 B.C.	Philip II of Macedonia conquers Thrace.
c. 200 B.C.	The Romans invade Thrace and make it part of their empire.
A.D. 330	Roman emperor Constantine moves his capital from Rome to Byzantium, renamed Constantinople.
c. 500	The Slavs settle in Bulgaria.
c. 600	The Bulgars invade Slav land and gradually assimilate with the Slavs to become the first Bulgarians.
681	Bulgar Khan Asparuhk establishes the First Bulgarian Kingdom.
893–927	Simeon I rules Bulgaria, creating a golden age of art, literature, and trade.
1018	Bulgaria becomes part of the Byzantine Empire.
1186	Ivan I establishes the Second Bulgarian Kingdom.
1300s	The Ottoman Turks invade the Balkans from the Middle East and begin five centuries of rule in Bulgaria.

1453	Constantinople falls to the Turks, ending the Byzantine Empire.
1762	Father Paisiy of Hilendar writes his *Slavo-Bulgarian History*, a lightning rod for Bulgarian nationalism.
1876	The April Uprising, last of the rebellions of the Bulgarians against the Turks is quelled and the Turks retaliate with "the Bulgarian atrocities."
1877–1878	The Russo-Turkish War ends with Bulgaria becoming an autonomous republic within the Ottoman Empire.
1908	German prince Ferdinand is crowned king of Bulgaria and begins to industrialize the country.
1912	The First Balkan War ends in full defeat of the Ottoman Turks.
1913	Bulgaria loses the Second Balkan War against Greece, Romania, and Montenegro.
1915–1918	Bulgaria sides with Germany and Austria-Hungary in World War I and ends up again on the losing side.
1919	The Bulgarian Agrarian National Union (BANU) comes to power under the leadership of Alexander Stambuliski.
1923	Opponents stage a coup and Stambuliski is assassinated.
1934	The government is seized by Zveno, a fascist-backed political coalition.
1935	Boris III becomes royal dictator of Bulgaria.
1941	Bulgaria signs the Tripartite Pact with Germany and Italy and becomes their reluctant ally in World War II.
1943	Boris dies under mysterious circumstances. His six-year-old son Simeon II ascends the throne.
1944	The Soviet Union declares war on Bulgaria and overruns the country.
1946	A Communist government headed by Georgi Dimitrov takes over Bulgaria.

1949	Dimitrov dies and is replaced by Joseph Stalin's protégé Vulko Chervenko.
1954	Todor Zhivkov is made first secretary of the Bulgarian Communist Party one year after Stalin's death.
1962	Zhivkov's rise to power in Bulgaria is complete; he is named premier.
1965	A coup against Zhivkov fails.
1968	Bulgaria sends troops to assist the Soviets in their invasion of Czechoslovakia.
1971	A new constitution solidifies the power of the Communists in Bulgaria.
1981	Bulgaria celebrates its 1,300th anniversary as a nation.
1984–1987	Zhivkov's campaign of forced assimilation for ethnic Turks leads to a mass exodus of over 300,000 Turks from Bulgaria.

1989

November	Five thousand people march on the National Assembly in the largest unofficial demonstration in over four decades. A week later Todor Zhivkov resigns after 35 years in power.
December	The United Democratic Front (UDF), a coalition of 16 political organizations is formed.

1990

January	The Communists agree to negotiations with the UDF. Zhivkov is arrested and charged with crimes against the Bulgarian people.
June	The first free and open parliamentary elections in more than 40 years take place and the Socialists, former Communists, win a majority of seats.
August	President Petar Mladenov resigns and is replaced by UDF leader Zhelyu Zhelev.

1991

October	UDF is the big winner in new parliamentary elections.
November	Filip Dimitrov forms a new coalition government.

1992

December	The Dimitrov government resigns under attack for ruining the economy. A new government is formed by another reformer, Lyuben Berov.

1994

September	Berov, also unable to improve conditions, resigns. The Socialist Party wins new elections. Zhan Videnov becomes prime minister.

1996

November	UDF leader Petar Stoyanov is elected president.
December	Videnov resigns as prime minister under a barrage of criticism.

1997

January	Demonstrators storm the National Assembly, trapping legislators inside. Police break up the barricade in a bloody melee. Demonstrations continue for weeks.
February	The Socialists agree to step down and new elections are scheduled for April; President Stoyanov appoints a caretaker government with Sofia mayor Stefan Sofiyanski as premier.
April	UDF is the big winner in parliamentary elections; a new coalition government is formed under the leadership of economist Ivan Kostov.

July	A crash program to stabilize the economy goes into effect and includes tighter government monetary control and the privatization of state banks.
August	Bulgarian naval forces participate in NATO's Partnership for Peace military exercises in Ukraine with several other Eastern European countries, Turkey, and the United States.

1998

August	Todor Zhivkov dies at age 86.

Further Reading

Nonfiction Books

Burt, Olive M. *Our World: Bulgaria* (New York: Julian Messner, 1970). An outdated introduction for children to Bulgaria and its people.

Curtiss, Glenn E., ed. *Bulgaria; A Country Study* (Washington, D.C.: Library of Congress, 1993). A comprehensive survey of contemporary Bulgaria, probably too detailed for most young adults, but well worth a perusal.

Resnick, Abraham. *Bulgaria* (Chicago: Children's Press, 1995). A good young adult introduction to Bulgaria, past and present, part of the excellent Enchantment of the World series.

Stavreva, Kirilka. *Bulgaria* (New York: Marshall Cavendish, 1997). Another good young adult introduction to the country and people, well illustrated, with the emphasis on culture and society rather than contemporary political events.

Fiction, Poetry, and Folklore

Naughton, James, editor. *Eastern and Central Europe: Traveller's Literary Companion* (Chicago: Passport Books, 1996). Excellent guide and introduction to the literature of Bulgaria and other Eastern European countries, with brief excerpts from the work of important writers.

Nicoloff, Assen. *Bulgarian Folklore* (Cleveland: published by the author, 1983). A comprehensive, academic study of Bulgarian folklore with many examples of folk beliefs and customs, folk songs, folktales, and proverbs.

Pridham, Radost. *A Gift from the Heart: Folk Tales from Bulgaria* (Cleveland: World Publishing Co., 1967). An enchanting collection of Bulgarian folktales, retold by a writer who was raised in Bulgaria.

Sapinkopf, Lisa, and Belv, Georgi, eds. *Clay and Star: Contemporary Bulgarian Poets* (Minneapolis: Milkweed Editions, 1992). An excellent cross section of poets and representative poems, many of them accessible to young adults.

Vazov, Ivan. *Under the Yoke* (New York: Twayne, 1971). The best-known Bulgarian novel in the West by one of Bulgaria's most-beloved authors. It portrays events in one village leading up to the 1896 April Uprising against the Turks. Vazov's characters are two-dimensional, his plot contrived and melodramatic, but the insights into Bulgarian village life near the end of Turkish rule are intriguing.

Index

Entries are filed letter by letter. **Boldface** page numbers indicate main discussion of topic; *italic* numbers indicate illustrations; page numbers followed by *c* indicate chronology; those followed by *m* indicate maps.